ALEXANDER PUSHKIN

A JOURNEY TO ARZRUM

translated by

Birgitta Ingemanson

Ardis

This translation is dedicated

to

Ron E. Openshaw

Contents

A JOURNEY TO ARZRUM

Preface

Recently I happened upon a book which was printed in Paris last year (1834) under the title *Voyages en Orient entrepris par ordre du Gouvernement Français.* The author, in giving his own account of the campaign of 1829, ends his discussion with the following words:

"Un poète distingué par son imagination a trouvé dans tant de hauts faits dont il a été témoin non le sujet d'un poème, mais celui d'une satyre."

As for the poets in the Turkish campaign, I knew only of A. S. Khomyakov and A. N. Muravyov. Both were in Count Dibich's army. The former wrote some fine lyric poems at the time; the latter reflected upon his journey to the Holy Land, which had produced such a strong impression. But I have not read any satire on the Arzrum campaign.

I would never have imagined that this was a reference to me, if in that very book I had not found my name among the names of the generals of the Detached Caucasus Corps. *"Parmi les chefs qui la commandaient (l'armée du Prince Paskewitch) on distinguait le Général Mouravief... le Prince Géorgien*

Tsitsevaze... le Prince Arménien Beboutof... le Prince Potemkine, le Général Raiewsky, et enfin—M. Pouchkine... qui avait quitté la capitale pour chanter les exploits de ses compatriotes."

I confess: these lines of the French traveler, despite their flattering epithets, vexed me more than the abuse of the Russian literary journals. *To seek inspiration* has always seemed to me a ridiculous and absurd fantasy: you cannot find inspiration; it, of itself, must find the poet. For me to go to a war intending to sing the praises of future exploits would be on the one hand quite arrogant, and on the other quite improper. I do not involve myself with military opinions. That is not my affair. Perhaps, the bold crossing over Sagan-Lu, a maneuver by which Count Paskevich cut the Seraskir off from Osman-Pasha, the defeat of two enemy corps in a single day, the swift march to Arzrum, all of this, which was crowned with complete success, is perhaps extremely worthy of ridicule in the eyes of military men (such as, for example, Mr. Commercial Consul Fantanier, the author of the journey to the Orient); but I would be ashamed to write satires on a famed Commander who received me affectionately in the shelter of his tent and found the time amidst his great concerns to accord me flattering attention. A person who has no need of the protection of the mighty values their good-will and hospitality, for there is nothing else he can ask of them. An accusation of ingratitude ought not to be left unanswered, as if it were worthless criticism or literary abuse. This is why I have decided to print this preface and publish my travel notes, as *all* that I have written about the campaign of 1829.

A. Pushkin

George Dawe, portrait of A. P. Ermolov

Chapter One

The Steppes. A Kalmyk Tent. The Caucasus Spas. The Georgian Military Highway. Vladikavkaz. An Ossetian Funeral. The Terek. The Darial Pass. Crossing the Snowcapped Mountains. The First Glimpse of Georgia. Aqueducts. Khozrev-Mirza. The Mayor of Dushet.

...From Moscow I went to Kaluga, Belev and Orel, and added thereby an extra two hundred versts; however, I did manage to see Ermolov. He lives in Orel, near which his estate is located. I called on him at eight in the morning and did not find him at home. The driver told me that Ermolov visited no one except his father, a simple, devout old man, and that the only people he did not receive were the town clerks, but that everyone else had free access to him. In an hour I called on him again. Ermolov received me with his usual cordiality. At first glance I did not find in him the least resemblance with his portraits, which are usually painted in profile. A round face, fiery gray eyes, bristly gray hair. The head of a tiger on the torso of Hercules. His smile is unpleasant, because it is not natural. But when he falls into thought and frowns, he becomes handsome and strikingly like the poetic portrait painted by Dawe. He was wearing a green Circassian jacket. On the walls of his study hung swords and daggers, mementoes of his rule in the Caucasus. It is obvious that he finds it hard to endure his inactivity. A few times he took to speaking of Paskevich and always scathingly; he would speak of his easy victories and compare him to Joshua, before whom the walls fell at the sound of a trumpet, and instead of referring to him as the Count of Èrivan' he would call him the Count of Jericho. "If he were to attack a stupid, inexperienced, but merely stubborn pasha, for example, the pasha who was in command at Shumla," said Ermolov, "that would be the end of Paskevich." I relayed to Ermolov Count Tolstoy's statement that Paskevich had done so well in the Persian campaign that the only way left for a clever man to distinguish himself would be to act slightly worse. Ermolov burst out laughing, but did not agree. "It would have been possible to save people and expense," he said. I think that he is writing, or wants to write, his memoirs. He is dissatisfied with Karamzin's *History;* he would like an ardent pen to describe the progress of the Russian people from insignificance to glory and power. Of Prince Kurbsky's writings he spoke *con amore.* He let the Germans have their due. "In about fifty years or so," he said, "people will think that in the present campaign there was an auxiliary Prussian or

Austrian army, presided over by some German generals or other." I stayed with him for about two hours. He was vexed at not remembering my full name. He kept apologizing with compliments. Several times the conversation touched on literature. Of Griboedov's verse he says that his jaw aches when he reads it. Of government and politics there was not a word.

My route was to take me through Kursk and Kharkov; but I turned off onto the direct road to Tiflis, thereby sacrificing a good dinner in a Kursk tavern (which is no mean trifle in our journeys); what is more, I did not have enough curiosity to visit the University of Kharkov, which is not nearly so tempting as the Kursk taverns.

The roads to Elets are terrible. Several times my carriage got stuck in mud, which was fully the equal of Odessa mud. Sometimes I covered no more than fifty versts in twenty-four hours. Finally I saw the Voronezh steppes and rolled easily over the green plain. In Novocherkask I found Count Pushkin, also on his way to Tiflis, and we agreed to travel together.

The transition from Europe to Asia is more perceptible with every hour: the forests disappear, the hills level out, the grass gets thicker and the vegetation richer; birds appear which are unknown in our forests; eagles sit on the hillocks that line the main road, as if on guard, and look proudly at the traveler; over lush pastures

> *Herds of indomitable mares*
> *Wander proudly.*

The Kalmyks settle around the station shacks. Their ugly, shaggy horses, known to you from Orlovsky's fine drawings, graze around their tents.

The other day I visited a Kalmyk tent (a wicker frame, covered with thick white felt). The whole family was about to have lunch. A cauldron was boiling in the middle, and the smoke was escaping through an opening at the top of the tent. A young Kalmyk girl, quite pretty, was sewing, and smoking tobacco. I sat down beside her. "What's your name?"–***–"How old are you?"–"Ten and eight."–"What are you sewing?"–"Trouser."–"For whom?"–"For self." She handed me her pipe and began to eat. Tea was boiling in the cauldron with mutton fat and salt. She offered me her ladle. I could not refuse and swallowed a mouthful, trying not to take a breath. I do not think that the cuisine of any other people could produce anything more repulsive. I asked for something with which to get rid of the taste. They gave me a small piece of dried mare's meat; I was happy even for that. Kalmyk coquetry frightened me; I hurried out of the tent–and rode off from the Circe of the Steppes.

In Stavropol I saw on the horizon the clouds that had so impressed me exactly nine years before. They were still the same, still in the same spot. These are the snowcapped peaks of the Caucasian chain.

From Georgievsk I went by to visit Goryachie Vody. Here I found great change: in my time the baths were in hastily built shacks. The springs, for the most part in their primitive state, gushed out, steamed and flowed down the mountains in various directions, leaving white and reddish traces behind them. We scooped the seething water with a ladle made of bark or the bottom of a broken bottle. Now magnificent baths and buildings have been erected. A boulevard lined by young lindens runs along the slope of Mount Mashuk. Everywhere there are neatly kept pathways, green benches, rectangular flowerbeds, little bridges, pavilions. The springs have been refined, lined with stone; nailed up on the walls of the bathhouses are lists of instructions from the police; everything is orderly, neat, prettified...

I confess: the Caucasus spas offer more conveniences nowadays; but I missed their former wild state; I missed the steep stone paths, the bushes and the unfenced cliffs over which I used to clamber. With sadness I left the spas, and set out on my way back to Georgievsk. Soon night fell. The clear sky was studded with millions of stars. I was riding along the bank of the Podkumok. Here A. Raevsky used to sit with me, listening to the melody of the waters. The majestic Beshtu stood outlined blacker and blacker in the distance, surrounded by mountains, its vassals, and finally it disappeared in the darkness...

The next day we continued and arrived in Ekaterinograd, formerly the seat of the military governor.

The Georgian Military Highway begins in Ekaterinograd; the post road ends. One hires horses to Vladikavkaz. A convoy of Cossacks and infantry soldiers is given, and one cannon. The mail leaves twice a week and the travelers join up: this is called an *opportunity.* We did not have to wait long. The mail arrived the next day, and the third morning at nine we were ready to set out. The whole caravan, consisting of five hundred people or thereabouts, assembled at a meeting-place. There was a drum roll. We were off. The cannon preceded, surrounded by infantry soldiers. Behind it stretched a long line of carriages, brichkas, and the hooded carts of the soldiers' wives, who were transferring from one fortress to another; behind them the train of two-wheeled carts began to creak. On either side ran herds of horses and oxen. Around them galloped

Nogai tribesmen in felt cloaks and with lassos. At first I greatly enjoyed all this, but it soon bored me. The cannon moved at a slow pace, the wick was smoking, and the soldiers lit their pipes from it. The slow pace of our march (on the first day we covered only fifteen versts), the unbearable heat, the scarcity of provisions, the restless stopovers for the night, and finally the continuous creaking of the Nogai carts made me lose patience. The Tartars pride themselves on this creaking, and say that they travel about like honest people, who have no need to hide. On this occasion it would have been more agreeable for me to journey in not quite so respectable company. The road is rather monotonous: a plain; on either side hills. On the horizon—the peaks of the Caucasus, which every day appear higher and higher. Fortresses, good enough for this region, with surrounding trenches, which in the old days each of us could have jumped over without running; with rusty cannon, which have not fired since the days of Count Gudovich; and crumbling ramparts, on which garrisons of chickens and geese roam. In the fortresses there are some shacks where with difficulty one can obtain a dozen eggs and some sour milk.

The first place of note is the Minaret fortress. On the way to it, our caravan went through a delightful valley between burial mounds, overgrown with linden and planetrees. These are the graves of several thousand who died from the plague. They were dotted with many-colored flowers which had sprung up from the infected dust. The snowy Caucasus gleamed to the right; an enormous wooded mountain rose before us; beyond it lay the fortress. All about it one can see traces of a ruined aul, which used to be called Tartartub and was in its time the main village in Great Kabarda. The slender, solitary minaret bears witness to the existence of the now vanished settlement. It rises gracefully between heaps of stones, on the bank of a dried-up stream. The inner stairway has not yet collapsed. I climbed it to the platform, from which the mullah's voice resounds no more. There I found several unknown names scratched in the bricks by fame-seeking travelers.

Our route became picturesque. The mountains towered above us. On their peaks one could make out barely visible flocks, crawling about like insects. We could also make out a shepherd who might have been a Russian and who, once taken prisoner, had grown old in his captivity. We came on more burial mounds, more ruins. Two or three grave monuments stood on the side of the road. In accordance with the custom of the Circassians, their horsemen are buried there. A Tartar inscription, an image of a sword, a brandmark, all

carved on the stone, have been left to predatory grandsons in memory of a predatory
ancestor.

The Circassians hate us. We have forced
them out of their free and spacious pasture-
lands; their auls are in ruins, whole tribes have
been annihilated. As time goes on, they move
deeper into the mountains, and direct their
raids from there. Friendship with the *peaceful* Circassians is unreliable: they are always
ready to aid their rebellious fellow tribesmen.
The spirit of their wild chivalry has declined
noticeably. They rarely attack the Cossacks
in equal number, and never the infantry; and
they flee when they see a cannon. Even so
they never pass up an opportunity to attack a
weak detachment or a defenseless person. The
area is full of rumors of their villainies. There
is almost no way of pacifying them, save by
disarming them, as the Crimean Tartars were
disarmed, which is extremely difficult to accomplish because of the hereditary feuds
among them and the blood vengeance. The
dagger and the sword are parts of their body,
and an infant begins to master them before
he can prattle. For them killing is a simple
bodily motion. Captives are kept in the hope
of ransom, but they are treated with horrible
inhumanity, forced to work beyond their
strength, fed with raw dough, beaten at will,
and guarded by their boys who at a single

word have the right to hack them with their childish swords. Recently a peaceful Circassian who had shot at a soldier was captured. He tried to justify himself by saying that his rifle had been loaded for too long. What can one do with such people? One must hope, however, that our annexation of the eastern region of the Black Sea, by cutting the Circassians off from trade with Turkey, will force them to become more friendly with us. The influence of luxury may favor their taming: the samovar would be an important innovation. There is, however, a stronger means, one more moral, more in keeping with the enlightenment of our time: the preaching of the Gospel. The Circassians accepted the Mohammedan faith very recently. They were attracted by the active fanaticism of the apostles of the *Koran,* among whom Mansur, an extraordinary man who had long incited the Caucasus against Russian rule, distinguished himself, and who was finally caught by us and died in the Solovetsky Monastery. The Caucasus awaits Christian missionaries. But instead of the living word, it is easier for our lassitude to pour forth dead letters and send mute books to people who are illiterate.

We reached Vladikavkaz, formerly Kapkai, the threshold of the mountains. It is surrounded by Ossetian auls. I visited one of them and found myself at a funeral. People were

crowding around a saklya. Outside stood two
oxen harnessed to a cart. The relatives and
friends of the deceased were assembling from
all directions and were entering the saklya,
weeping loudly and beating their foreheads
with their fists. The women stood by quietly.
They carried out the corpse on a felt cloak...

> *...like a warrior taking his rest*
> *With his martial cloak around him,*

they laid him in the cart. One of the guests
took the dead man's rifle, blew the powder
from the pan, and laid it alongside the body.
The oxen started off. The guests rode after.
The body was to be buried in the mountains,
some thirty versts from the aul. Unfortunately,
no one could explain these rituals to me.

The Ossets are the poorest tribe of all the
peoples who inhabit the Caucasus; their women
are beautiful and, as one hears, very well dis-
posed to travelers. At the gate of the fortress
I met the wife and daughter of an imprisoned
Osset man. They were bringing him his dinner.
Both seemed calm and brave; however, at my
approach both bowed their heads and covered
themselves with their tattered *yashmaks*. In
the fortress I saw Circassian hostages, spirited
and handsome boys. They are constantly
playing tricks and escaping from the fortress.
They are kept in a sorry state. They go about

in rags, half naked, and in appalling filth. On some of them I saw wooden shackles. It is very likely that the hostages, once released, do not miss their stay in Vladikavkaz.

The cannon left us. We set out with the infantry and the Cossacks. The Caucasus received us into its sanctuary. We heard the muffled roar and caught sight of the Terek, which was pouring forth in several directions. We traveled along its left bank. Its noisy waves move the wheels of the low little Ossetian mills which look like dog kennels. The farther we penetrated into the mountains, the narrower the pass became. The confined Terek throws its turbid waves with a roar over the cliffs which block its path. The pass winds along its course. At their rocky base the mountains have been ground smooth by its waves. I went along on foot and kept stopping, overwhelmed by the gloomy beauty of nature. The weather was bleak; the clouds were stretched heavily around the black peaks. Count Pushkin and Stjernvall, as they watched the Terek, reminisced about Imatra and gave preference to *"the thundering river in the North."* But I had nothing with which to compare the spectacle before me.

Before we reached Lars, I dropped behind the convoy, having lost myself in contemplation over the enormous cliffs, between which the Terek beats with indescribable fury.

Suddenly a soldier runs up to me, shouting to me from afar: "Don't stop, your Excellency, they'll kill you!" Unexpected as indeed it was, this warning seemed extremely strange to me. The fact is that Ossetian bandits, safe in this confined terrain, shoot at travelers across the Terek. The day before we crossed, they had attacked General Bekovich this way, who, however, galloped past as they shot at him. On the cliff one can see the ruins of some castle: they are cluttered with the saklyas of peaceful Ossets, like swallows' nests.

In Lars we stopped to spend the night. Here we found a French traveler who frightened us with the road ahead. He advised us to leave our carriages behind in Kobi and continue on horseback. It was with him that for the first time we drank Kakhetinsky wine out of a stinking *wineskin,* recalling the feasting in the *Iliad:*

And in goat-skins wine, our joy!

Here I found a soiled copy of *The Prisoner of the Caucasus,* and, I confess, reread it with great pleasure. It is all weak, young, incomplete; but a great deal was intuited and expressed aptly.

In the morning we continued on. Turkish prisoners were working on the road. They complained about the food that was given them. They could just not get used to Russian black bread. This reminded me of the words of my friend Sheremetiev, on his return from Paris: "It's terrible, brother, to live in Paris: there's nothing to eat; you can't get hold of black bread!"

Seven versts from Lars is the Darial post. The pass bears the same name. The cliffs stand like parallel walls on both sides. It is so narrow here, so narrow, writes one traveler, that you not only see, but, it would seem, you feel the closeness. A patch of the sky shows blue, like a ribbon, over your head. Streams falling from the height of the mountain in shallow and splashing spurts reminded me of the Abduction of Ganimed, that strange painting by Rembrandt. Besides, the light in the pass is completely in his style. In certain places the Terek washes against the very foot of the cliffs, and rocks are heaped up on the road like a dam. Not far from the post a little bridge is boldly thrown across the river. When you stand on it, it is as if you were in a mill. The whole bridge shakes, and the Terek roars like the wheels that move the millstones. Opposite Darial on a steep cliff one can see the ruins of a fortress. Tradition has it that it was the hiding-place of a certain Queen Daria, who gave her name to the pass: a legend. Darial means gate in ancient Persian. According to the testimony of Pliny, the Gate of the

Caucasus, which was erroneously called the Caspian Gate, was located here. The pass was locked with a real gate, made of wood, fitted with iron. Under it, writes Pliny, flows the river Diriodoris. A fortress was also erected here to restrain the raids of the wild tribes; and so on. See the journey of Count J. Potocki, whose scholarly research is as entertaining as his Spanish novels.

From Darial we set out for Kazbek. We saw the *Trinity Gate* (an arch, formed in the cliff by a powder explosion)—the road used to run beneath it, but now the Terek which so often changes its bed flows through there.

Not far from the settlement of Kazbek we crossed over the *Furious Gorge,* a ravine which during heavy downpours turns into a raging stream. At this time it was completely dry, and roaring in name only.

The village Kazbek is located at the foot of Mount Kazbek and belongs to Prince Kazbek. The prince, a man of about forty-five, is taller than the pivot-man of the Preobrazhensky Regiment. We found him in the *dukhan* (that is the name for Georgian taverns, which are much poorer and dirtier than the Russian ones). In the door lay a big-bellied wineskin (ox fur), spreading its four legs wide. The giant squeezed some *chikhir'* wine out of it and asked me some questions which I answered with the respect due his rank and size. We parted great friends.

Soon one's impressions are dulled. Hardly a day had gone by, and the roar of the Terek and its monstrous waterfalls, its cliffs and precipices no longer attracted my attention. An impatience to reach Tiflis completely overpowered me. I went past Kazbek as indifferently as I once sailed past Chatyrdag. It is also true that the rainy and foggy weather prevented me from seeing its snowy mass, which in the expression of a poet "holds up the horizon."

A Persian prince was expected. At some distance from Kazbek we happened to meet some carriages which made passage on the narrow road difficult. As the vehicles passed the convoy officer announced to us that he was accompanying a Persian court poet, and at my request introduced me to Fazil-Khan. With the help of an interpreter I was about to start a bombastic Oriental greeting; but how humiliated I felt, when Fazil-Khan answered my inappropriate inventiveness with the simple, intelligent courtesy of a gentleman! "He hoped to see me in Petersburg; he was sorry that our acquaintance would be of short duration, and so on." With shame I was forced to abandon my pompously jocular tone and come down to ordinary European phrases. That was a lesson for our Russian tendency to make fun of others. In the future I shall not judge a person by his sheep-skin *papakha** and painted nails.

The post of Kobi is located at the very foot of the Mountain of the Cross, over which we now had to go. We stopped there to spend the night and began to think of how to accomplish this awesome feat: should we leave the carriages, and mount the Cossacks' horses, or send for Ossetian oxen? To be on the safe side, I wrote an official petition in the name of all of our caravan to Mr. Chilyaev, who was in charge out here, and we went to sleep expecting carts.

The next day about noon we heard noise, shouts, and saw an unusual spectacle: eighteen pairs of scraggly, undersized oxen, driven on by a crowd of half naked Ossets, were with difficulty dragging along the light Viennese carriage of my friend O***. This spectacle at once disspelled all my doubts. I decided to send my heavy Petersburg carriage back to Vladikavkaz and to ride to Tiflis on horseback. Count Pushkin did not want to follow my example. He preferred to harness a whole herd of oxen to his brichka, which was loaded with supplies of every kind, and ride in triumph over the snowy ridge. We parted, and I set out with Colonel Ogarev, who was inspecting the local roads.

---

* This is what Persian caps are called.

31

A Journey to Arzrum

The road went through a landslide which had fallen at the end of June, 1827. Such accidents usually happen every seven years. An enormous block fell down, burying the pass for a whole verst and damming the Terek. Sentries who were standing further down heard a terrible thunder and saw that the river had quickly become shallow and in a quarter of an hour completely silent and drained. The Terek was unable to burst through the landslide for two hours. But then it was terrifying!

We were climbing straight up, higher and higher. Our horses got stuck in the loose snow, under which little streams could be heard. I looked at the road in amazement and could not understand how it could be possible to ride over it on wheels.

At this time I heard a muffled thunder. "That's an avalanche," said Mr. Ogarev to me. I looked around and saw not far off a heap of snow which was crumbling and slowly sliding down the steep mountain side. Small avalanches are not rare here. Last year a Russian driver was going along the Mountain of the Cross. An avalanche broke off; an awesome mass fell down on his vehicle; it swallowed wagon, horse and peasant, rolled across the road and down into the precipice with its booty. We reached the very top of the mountain. A granite cross stands there, an old monument repaired by Ermolov.

The travelers usually get out of their carriages and walk there. Recently some foreign consul came by: he was so weak that he demanded to be blindfolded; he was led by the arm, and when the bandage was removed, he got down on his knees, thanked God, and so on, which greatly astonished the guides.

The instantaneous transition from awesome Caucasus to lovely Georgia is enchanting. The air of the South suddenly starts to waft over the traveler. From the height of Mount Gut the Kaishaur Valley opens up with its inhabited cliffs, its orchards, and its bright Aragva, which winds like a silver ribbon—and all this in a reduced scale, at the bottom of a three-verst-high precipice along which the dangerous road goes.

We were descending into the valley. A new moon appeared in the clear sky. The evening air was quiet and warm. I spent the night on the bank of the Aragva, in Mr. Chilyaev's home. The next day I parted from my amiable host and continued on my way.

Georgia begins here. Bright valleys watered by the merry Aragva replaced the gloomy gorges and the awesome Terek. Instead of bare cliffs I saw green mountains and fruit-trees around me. Aqueducts gave evidence of the presence of civilization. One of them struck me with its perfect optical illusion:

the water seems to run uphill.

In Paisanaur I stopped to change horses. There I met a Russian officer who was accompanying the Persian prince. Soon after I heard the sound of little bells, and a whole line of *katars* (mules), tied one to the other and packed in the Asian manner, dragged itself along the road. I set out on foot without waiting for the horses; and at half a verst from Ananur, where the road turns, I met Khozrev-Mirza. His vehicles were standing still. He personally looked out of his carriage and nodded to me. A few hours after our meeting some mountaineers attacked the Prince. When he heard the whistle of bullets, Khozrev leapt out of his carriage, mounted a horse and galloped off. The Russians who were with him were amazed at his courage. The fact is that the young Asian, not being used to a carriage, regarded it as a trap rather than a refuge.

I got to Ananur, feeling no tiredness. My horses had not arrived. I was told that the town of Dushet was no more than ten versts away, so I set out on foot again. But I did not know that the road went uphill. Those ten versts were worth a good twenty.

Evening fell; I went ahead, all the time climbing higher and higher. To lose one's way was impossible; but in places the muddy clay, formed by springs, reached up to my knees. I got completely exhausted. The darkness increased. I heard the howling and barking of dogs and was glad, imagining that the town was not far away. But I was mistaken: it was the Georgian shepherd dogs barking, and jackals, not unusual beasts in that area, howling. I cursed my impatience, but there was nothing I could do. Finally I caught sight of lights, and around midnight I found myself near houses surrounded by trees. The first person I met volunteered to take me to the mayor, for which he demanded an *abaz* from me.

My appearance at the mayor's, an old Georgian officer, produced great commotion. First, I demanded a room, where I could undress; second, a glass of wine; third, an abaz for my guide. The mayor did not know how to receive me, and looked at me incredulously. Seeing that he was in no hurry to carry out my requests, I began to take my cloak off in front of him, asking his pardon *de la liberté grande.* Fortunately, in my pocket I found the order for posthorses proving that I was a peaceful traveler, and not Rinaldo-Rinaldini. That blessed document had an immediate effect: a room was assigned to me, a glass of wine was brought, and an abaz given to my guide along with a fatherly reprimand for his venality, demeaning to Georgian hospitality. I threw myself down on the sofa, hoping to fall into a heroic sleep after my deed: but there was no chance of that! fleas, far more dangerous than jackals, attacked me and gave me no peace the whole night. In the morning my man came to me and announced that Count Pushkin had safely crossed the snowy mountains with the oxen and arrived in Dushet. I had to hurry! Count Pushkin and Stjernvall visited me and suggested that we again continue together. I left Dushet with the pleasant thought that I would spend the night in Tiflis.

The road was as pleasant and picturesque, although we seldom saw any signs of habitation. A few versts from Gartsiskal we crossed the Kura river on an ancient bridge, a monument of the Roman campaigns, and rode at an even trot, and sometimes even gallop, toward Tiflis where we arrived unnoticed at about eleven at night.

Chapter Two

I put up at an inn, and the next day I set out for the celebrated Tiflis baths. The city seemed well-populated to me. The Asian-style buildings and the bazaar reminded me of Kishinev. Along the narrow and steep streets ran donkeys carrying double baskets; oxen harnessed to carts blocked the way. Armenians, Georgians, Circassians, Persians thronged in the irregular square; among them were young Russian officials, riding around on Karabakh stallions. At the entrance to the bathhouse sat the owner, an elderly Persian. He opened the door for me, I went into a spacious room, and what did I see? More than fifty women, young and old, half-dressed and completely undressed, sitting and standing, were undressing and dressing on the benches which were placed along the walls. I stopped. "Come on, come on," said the owner to me, "today is Tuesday: Women's Day. It doesn't matter, no harm."—"Of course no harm," I answered him, "on the contrary." The appearance of men produced no impression. They continued to laugh and talk among themselves. Not one hurried to cover herself with her yashmak; not one stopped undressing. It seemed that I had entered like an invisible being. Many of them were genuinely beautiful, and justified the imagination of T. Moore:

> *a lovely Georgian maid,*
> *With all the bloom, the freshen'd glow*
> *Of her own country maiden's looks,*
> *When warm they rise from Teflis' brooks*

Lalla Rookh

On the other hand I know nothing more repulsive than the old women in Georgia—they are witches.

The Persian took me into the baths: a hot, iron-sulphurous spring was pouring into a deep tub hewn out of the cliff. Never in my life have I encountered either in Russia or in Turkey anything more luxurious than the Tiflis baths. I'll describe them in detail.

The owner left me in the care of a Tartar bathhouse attendant. I must confess that he had no nose; this did not prevent him from being a master of his trade. Hassan (that was the noseless Tartar's name) began by laying me out on the warm stone floor; after which he began to beat my limbs, stretch my joints, and pummel me violently with his fist; I did not feel the least pain, but an amazing relaxation. (Asian bathhouse attendants sometimes go into ecstasy, and jump up on your shoulders, slide with their feet over your thighs, and dance squatting on your back, *e sempre bene.*) After this he rubbed me for a long time with a woolen mitten, and having splattered me generously with warm water, began to wash me with a soaped linen bag. It is an indescribable sensation: the hot soap pours over you like air! NB: the woolen mitten and linen bag ought definitely to be adopted in Russian baths: connoisseurs will be grateful for such an innovation.

After the bag, Hassan let me into the tub; and with that the ceremony ended.

In Tiflis I hoped to find Raevsky, but after learning that his regiment was already on the march, I decided to ask Count Paskevich for permission to ride out to join up with the army.

I spent about two weeks in Tiflis and got acquainted with the local society. Sankovsky, the publisher of the *Tiflis Record,* told me many curious things about the area, about Prince Tsitsianov, about A. P. Ermolov, and so on. Sankovsky loves Georgia and foresees a brilliant future for it.

Georgia sought refuge as a Russian protectorate in 1783, which did not prevent glorious Aga-Mohammed from occupying and destroying Tiflis and carrying off 20,000 inhabitants as captives (1795). Georgia came under Emperor Alexander's scepter in 1802. The Georgians are a warlike people. They have proved their bravery under our banners. Their intellectual capabilities await further development. On the whole they are of a happy and sociable disposition. On holidays the men drink and carouse in the streets. The dark-eyed boys sing, jump about and somersault; the women dance the *lezginka*.

The music of Georgian songs is pleasant. One of them was translated for me word for word; I think it was composed quite recently; there is in it some Oriental nonsense, which has its poetic value. Here you are:

Soul, recently born in paradise! Soul, created for my happiness! from you, immortal, I await life.

From you, blossoming Spring, from you, two-week Moon, from you, my Guardian Angel, from you I await life.

Your face beams and you gladden with a smile. I do not want to possess the world; I want your glance. From you I await life.

Mountain rose, refreshed with dew! Chosen favorite of nature! Silent, secret treasure! from you I await life.

The Georgians drink, but not the way we
do, and are surprisingly strong. Their wines
do not travel well, and spoil quickly, but on
the spot they are fine. The Kakhetinsky and
Karabakh wines are the equal of some bur-
gundies. The wine is kept in *maranas,* enormous jugs, buried in the ground. They are
opened with festive rituals. Recently a Russian
dragoon who had secretly unearthed such a
jug fell in it and drowned in Kakhetinsky
wine, like the unfortunate Clarence in the
barrel of Malaga.

Tiflis is situated on the banks of the
Kura, in a valley surrounded by rocky mountains. These shelter it on all sides from the
winds, and when they grow hot in the sun
they do not warm, but scald the motionless
air. This is the reason for the unbearable hot-
spells that prevail in Tiflis, despite the fact
that the city is situated just under the forty-
first parallel. Its very name *(Tbilis-kalar)* means
Hot City.

A large part of the city is built in Asian
style: low buildings, flat roofs. Buildings with
European architecture are going up in the nor-
thern section, and around them regular squares
are beginning to appear. The bazaar is divided
into several rows; the shops are full of Turkish
and Persian goods, rather inexpensive if one
considers the generally high cost of living.
Tiflis weapons are highly praised throughout

the Orient. Count Samoylov and V., who were famed here for their heroic prowess, used to try out their new swords by cutting a sheep in two or chopping off the head of a bull with one blow.

In Tiflis Armenians constitute the main part of the population; in 1825 there were up to 2,500 families. During the present wars their number has increased even more. The number of Georgian families reaches 1,500. Russians do not consider themselves local residents. Military men, obedient to orders, live in Georgia because they have been so directed. Young titular councilors come here in pursuit of the coveted rank of assessor. The former and the latter look upon Georgia as exile.

The climate in Tiflis, they tell you, is unhealthy. The local fevers are awful; they are treated with mercury, which can be administered without harm because of the heat. The doctors feed it to their patients without any qualms. General Sipyagin died, they say, because his staff medic, who had come with him from Petersburg, became frightened of the dose suggested by the local doctors and did not give it to his patient. The local fevers resemble those of the Crimea and Moldavia and are treated in the same way.

The inhabitants drink the water of the Kura, muddy but pleasant. In all springs and

wells the water tastes strongly of sulphur.
However, wine is in such general use here
that a lack of water would go unnoticed.

In Tiflis I was surprised to see how little
money was worth. After I had traversed two
streets in a cab and let it go in half an hour,
I had to pay two silver rubles. I thought at
first that the driver was taking advantage of a
newcomer's ignorance; but I was told that this
was the proper amount. Everything else is expensive in proportion.

We went to the German colony and had
dinner there. We drank beer which is made
there, with a very unpleasant taste, and paid
very much for a very bad dinner. In my inn
the food was just as expensive and poor. General Strekalov, a famous epicure, once invited
me to dinner; unfortunately they served the
dishes according to rank at his house, and
there were English officers wearing general's
epaulettes at the table. The servants passed
me by with such zeal that I got up from the
table hungry. The Devil take that Tiflis
epicure!

I impatiently awaited the resolution of
my fortune. Finally I received a note from
Raevsky. He wrote urging me to hurry to Kars,
because in a few days the army was to continue on. I left the very next day.

I went on horseback, changing horses at

the Cossack posts. The earth around me was scorched by the heat. From afar the Georgian villages seemed to me to be beautiful gardens, but as I rode up to them I saw a few poor saklyas lying in the shade of dusty poplars. The sun had set, but the air was still stifling:

> *Burning nights!*
> *Alien stars!...*

The moon was shining; all was quiet; only the tread of my horse resounded in the nocturnal stillness. I rode for a long time without encountering any sign of habitation. Finally I caught sight of a solitary saklya. I began to knock at the door. The owner came out. I asked for some water first in Russian, then in Tartar. He did not understand me. What amazing indifference! Thirty versts from Tiflis on the road to both Persia and Turkey, he did not know a word either of Russian or Tartar.

After spending the night at a Cossack post I continued on at dawn. The road went through mountains and forest. I met traveling Tartars; there were some women among them. They sat straddling their horses, wrapped in yashmaks; all one could see were their eyes and the heels of their shoes.

I began the ascent of Bezobdal, the mountain which separates Georgia from ancient Armenia. A wide road shaded by trees

winds around the mountain. On the peak of Bezobdal I passed through a small gorge called,
it seems, the Wolf's Gate, and found myself
on the natural border of Georgia. New mountains rose before me, a new horizon; below
me spread fertile green wheatfields. I glanced
once more at scorched Georgia, and began to
descend: along the sloping side of the mountain toward the fresh plains of Armenia. With
indescribable pleasure I noticed that the heat
had suddenly decreased: the climate was
already different.

My man lagged behind with the pack
horses. I rode alone in the flowering wilderness surrounded by mountains in the distance.
Absentmindedly I rode past the post where I
was to have changed horses. More than six
hours went by and I began to be surprised at
how long it was taking between stations. Off
to one side I saw piles of rocks resembling
native saklyas and set off toward them. Indeed,
I arrived at an Armenian village. A few
women in colorful rags were sitting on the flat
roof of an underground saklya. I made myself
understood somehow. One of them went
down into the saklya and brought me some
cheese and milk. Having rested a few minutes,
I set out again and saw opposite me on the
high bank of a river the fortress of Gergery.
Three streams plunged down the high bank
foaming noisily. I crossed the river. Two oxen

harnessed to a cart were descending the steep road. Some Georgians were accompanying the cart. "Where do you come from?" I asked them. "From Teheran."—"What do you have on your cart?"—*"Griboed."* This was the body of the slain Griboedov, which they were taking to Tiflis.

I did not believe I would ever meet our Griboedov again! I parted with him last year, in Petersburg, before his departure for Persia. He was sad, and had strange forebodings. I thought of reassuring him; he said to me: *"Vous ne connaissez pas ces gens-là; vous verrez qu'il faudra jouer des couteaux."* He assumed that bloodshed would result at the death of the Shah and the ensuing feuds among his seventy sons. But the aged Shah is still alive, and yet Griboedov's prophetic words came true. He fell under Persian daggers, a victim of ignorance and perfidy. His mutilated corpse, which had been the plaything of the Teheran rabble for three days, was recognized only by a hand, once pierced by a bullet.

I got to know Griboedov in 1817. His melancholy character, his caustic wit, his good nature, his very weaknesses and vices, those inevitable companions of mankind— everything in him was unusually appealing. Although born with ambition equal to his talents he was long trapped by petty needs and obscurity. The abilities of the statesman remained unapplied; the talent of the poet was not recognized; even his cold and brilliant courage were for some time under suspicion. Some friends knew his value and encountered that distrustful smile, that inane, unbearable smile— every time they would speak of him as an unusual person. People are convinced only by Fame and do not understand that among them there may be some Napoleon who has not commanded a single company of chasseurs, or another Descartes who has not published a single line in the *Moscow Telegraph*. Besides, our respect for Fame arises, perhaps, out of self-esteem: for our voice too must contribute to that Fame.

Griboedov's life was darkened by certain clouds: a consequence of fiery passions and powerful circumstances. He felt the necessity to settle accounts once and for all with his youth and make a definite break in his life. He bade farewell to Petersburg and idle carefreeness; he went to Georgia where he spent eight years in solitary, tireless pursuits. His return to Moscow in 1824 signalled a change in his fortunes and the start of continuous success. While still in manuscript his comedy *Woe from Wit* had an incredible effect and put him on a par with our leading poets. Some time later his thorough knowledge of the region where the war was starting opened up a new career for him; he was appointed ambassador. When he had arrived in Georgia, he married the one he loved... I do not know of anything more enviable than the final years of his stormy life. Even his death which befell him in the midst of a valiant, unequal battle, held nothing terrible, nothing agonizing for Griboedov. It was instantaneous and beautiful.

What a pity that Griboedov did not leave his memoirs! To write his biography should be the task of his friends; but our remarkable people disappear without leaving a trace. We are lazy and have no curiosity...

In Gergery I met Buturlin who like me was on his way to the army. Buturlin was traveling with every imaginable luxury. I dined with him as if we were in Petersburg. We decided to travel together; but the demon of impatience again possessed me. My man asked my permission to rest. I set out alone even without a guide. The road was the same the whole way and completely safe.

When I had crossed the mountain and descended into the tree-shaded valley, I caught sight of a mineral spring flowing across the road. There I met an Armenian priest on his way to Akhaltsyk from Erivan'. "What's new in Erivan'?" I asked him. —"In Erivan' they've got the plague," he answered, "and what's there to hear about Akhaltsyk?"—"In Akhaltsyk they've got the plague," I answered him.

Having exchanged these pleasant tidings, we parted.

I rode on amidst fertile wheatfields and blossoming meadows. The crop was swaying, waiting for the sickle. I was admiring the beautiful soil, the fertility of which is proverbial in the Orient. Toward evening I arrived in Pernike. There was a Cossack post. The sergeant was forecasting a storm and advised me to stay overnight, but I wanted to be certain to reach Gumry that day.

I was to cross through low mountains, the natural border of the Pashalic of Kars. The sky was covered with clouds; I was hoping that the wind, which increased now and then, would disperse them. But it started to drizzle and then the rain kept getting heavier. From Pernike to Gumry it is twenty-seven versts. I tightened the straps on my felt cloak, put the hood over my cap and entrusted myself to Providence.

More than two hours went by. The rain would not stop. The water flowed in little streams from my cloak which was heavy with the weight of the rain, and from the hood which was soaked. Finally a cold trickle began to make its way under my necktie, and soon the rain drenched me to the skin. The night was dark; a Cossack rode ahead pointing out the way. We began to go uphill; meanwhile the rain had stopped and the clouds had dispersed. There were still about ten versts left to Gumry. The wind, blowing freely, was so strong that it dried me completely in a quarter of an hour. I did not think that I would escape a fever. Finally I reached Gumry about midnight. The Cossack took me straight to the post. We stopped at a tent, which I hurried into. There I found twelve Cossacks sleeping one next to the other. I was given a place; I fell down on my cloak, completely unconscious from fatigue. That day I had covered seventy-five versts. I fell asleep as if I were dead.

The Cossacks woke me up at sunrise. My first thought was: have I got a fever. But I felt that I was in good spirits and well, thank God; there was no trace either of sickness or fatigue. I went out of the tent into the fresh morning air. The sun was rising. On the clear sky one could see a white-snowcapped, twin-peaked mountain. "What mountain is that?" I asked, stretching myself, and heard the answer: "That's Ararat." What a powerful effect a few syllables can have! Avidly I looked at the Biblical mountain, saw the ark moored to its peak with the hope of regeneration and life, saw both the raven and dove, flying forth, the symbols of punishment and reconciliation...

My horse was ready. I set out with a guide. It was a beautiful morning. The sun was shining. We rode along a wide meadow, through thick green grass sprinkled with dew and drops of the rain of the day before. In front of us glittered a small river over which we would have to cross. And there is the Arpachai, the Cossack told me. Arpachai! our border! This was as good as Ararat. I galloped toward the river with an indescribable feeling. I had never before seen foreign soil. The border held something mysterious for me; from childhood travels had been my cherished dream. For a long time I then led a nomadic life, wandering now around the South, now the North, and never before had I broken out from the borders of immense Russia. I rode happily into the sacred river, and my good horse carried me out on the Turkish bank. But this bank had already been conquered: I was still in Russia.

I still had seventy-five versts left to reach Kars. I hoped to see our camp by evening. I did not stop anywhere. Halfway, in an Armenian village, built in the mountains on the bank of a little river, instead of dinner I ate the cursed Armenian bread, *churek,* which is baked in the shape of a flat cake, half mixed with ashes, and for which the Turkish prisoners in the Darial Pass longed so. I would have given much for a piece of Russian black bread, which was so repulsive to them. I was accompanied by a young Turk who was a dreadful

51

chatterbox. All the way he babbled in Turkish, not worrying about if I understood him or not. I made every effort to pay attention and tried to make him out. I think he was berating the Russians, and having got used to seeing them all in uniforms took me for a foreigner because of my clothes. We happened to meet a Russian officer. He was on his way from our camp and told me that the army was already on the march from Kars. I cannot describe my despair: the thought that I would have to return to Tiflis getting uselessly exhausted in desolate Armenia absolutely killed me. The officer went his way; the Turk resumed his monologue; but I could not stand him now. I changed to a swift trot, and by evening arrived at a Turkish village, located twenty versts from Kars.

I dismounted and tried to enter the first saklya, but the owner appeared in the door and sent me away with curses. I answered his greeting with my whip. The Turk raised a cry; people gathered. It seemed to me that my guide stood up for me. A caravan-sarai was pointed out to me; I entered a big saklya, which resembled a cattle-shed; there was no place where I could spread out my cloak. I demanded a horse. The Turkish headman came to me. To all his incomprehensible words I answered one thing only: *verbana at* (give me a horse). The Turks would not agree. Finally

I got the idea of showing them money (with which I ought to have started). A horse was brought at once, and they gave me a guide.

I rode along a wide valley surrounded by mountains. Soon I saw Kars, which loomed white on one of them. My Turk kept pointing it out to me, repeating: *Kars, Kars!* and started to gallop; I followed him, tormented with worry: my fate was to be decided in Kars. There I was to find out where our camp was and if there was still any possibility for me to catch up with the army. Meanwhile the sky became covered with clouds and the rain started again; but I no longer worried about that.

We rode into Kars. As we rode up to the gate of the city I heard a Russian drum: they were sounding retreat. The guard took my note and went to the commandant. I stood in the rain for about half an hour. Finally they let me pass. I ordered my guide to take me straight to the baths. We rode along crooked and steep streets; our horses slipped on the bad Turkish pavement. We stopped at one building, of rather a bad appearance. This was the bathhouse. The Turk dismounted and began to knock at the door. Nobody answered. The rain was pouring down over me. Finally a young Armenian came out of a nearby house and after a discussion with my Turk called me over, expressing himself in rather pure Russian. He took me along a narrow staircase to the second floor of his house. In a room furnished with low sofas and threadbare carpets sat an old woman, his mother. She came up to me and kissed my hand. The son ordered her to light the fire and prepare supper for me. I took off my cloak and sat down in front of the fire. In came my host's younger brother, a lad of about seventeen. Both brothers had been in Tiflis and had each lived there for a few months. They told me that our army had left the day before, that our camp was twenty-five versts from Kars. I was completely reassured. Soon the old woman had cooked me some mutton with onions, which seemed to me the height of culinary art. We all lay down to sleep in the one room; I sprawled opposite the dying fire and fell asleep in the pleasant hope of seeing Count Paskevich's camp the next day.

In the morning I went to have a look at the city. The younger of my hosts undertook to be my cicerone. As I examined the fortifications and the citadel, which was built on an inaccessible cliff, I found it impossible to understand how we could have taken Kars. My Armenian explained to me as well as he could the military actions, of which he himself had been a witness. Since I noticed that he had particular eagerness for war, I suggested that he come out with me to visit the army. He agreed at once. I sent him for horses. He appeared with an officer who demanded a written order from me. Judging by the Asian features of his face, I did not deem it necessary to rummage around in my papers, but took out of my pocket the first piece of paper that I found. The officer scrutinized it with a self-important air and immediately ordered that his Excellency be brought horses according to the instructions, and gave me back my paper: this was a missive to the Kalmyk girl which I had scribbled off at one of the Cossack stations. In half an hour I rode out of Kars and Artemy (that was my Armenian's name) was already galloping beside me on a Turkish stallion, with a supple Kurdish javelin in his hand, a dagger in his belt, and dreaming about Turks and battles.

I rode over land everywhere sown with grain; villages were visible all around, but they were empty; the inhabitants had fled. The road was fine, and in marshy places paved — across the streams stone bridges had been built. There was a perceptible rise in the terrain—the first hills of the Sagan-Lu ridge, ancient Tauris, began to appear. About two hours went by; I rode up a sloping elevation and suddenly saw our camp, spread out on the bank of the Kars-chai; in a few minutes I was already in Raevsky's tent.

I. Aivazovsky, portrait of N. N. Raevsky

Chapter Three

The March over Sagan-Lu. Crossfire.Camp Life. The Battle with the Seraskir of Arzrum. A Saklya Demolished by an Explosion.

I arrived in time. On that very day (June 13) the army received the order to march forward. While dining at Raevsky's, I listened to the young generals, who were discussing the maneuver which had been scheduled for them. General Burtsov had been detached to the left along the great Arzrum road directly opposite the Turkish camp, while the rest of the army was to go along the right side around the enemy.

The army set out before five. I was riding with the Nizhegorod Dragoon Regiment, conversing with Raevsky whom I had not seen for some years. Night fell; we stopped in the valley where the whole army made an encampment. There I had the honor of being introduced to Count Paskevich.

I found the Count in his quarters before a bivouac fire, surrounded by his staff. He was cheerful and received me affably. Inexperienced in the military arts, I did not suspect that the fate of the campaign was being decided at that very moment. There I saw our

A Journey to Arzrum

Volkhovsky covered with dust from head to foot, with a full growth of beard, exhausted from worry. Nevertheless he found time to chat with me as an old comrade. There I also saw Mikhail Pushchin, who had been wounded the year before. He is loved and respected as a wonderful comrade and a brave soldier. Many of my old friends surrounded me. How they had changed! how fast time goes by!

> *Heu! fugaces, Posthume, Posthume,*
> *Labuntur anni...*

I returned to Raevsky and spent the night in his tent. In the middle of the night terrible shouts awoke me: one would have thought that the enemy had made an unexpected attack. Raevsky sent someone to find out the reason for the alarm: some Tartar horses had broken loose and were running around in camp, and the Moslems (that is how the Tartars who serve in our army are called) were trying to catch them.

At sunrise the army moved forward. We approached the mountains which were overgrown with forests. We rode into a ravine. The dragoons were saying to each other: "Look out, brother, take courage: they'll get you at once with caseshot." As a matter of fact it was favorable terrain for an ambush; but the Turks, diverted in the other direction by General Burtsov's maneuver, did not avail themselves of their advantages. We passed through the dangerous ravine safely and took our stand on the heights of Sagan-Lu ten versts from the enemy camp.

Nature around us was sullen. The air was cold, the mountains covered with sad pine-trees. Snow lay in the gorges.

> *...nec Armeniis in oris,*
> *Amice Valgi, stat glacies iners*
> *Menses per omnes...*

We had hardly time to rest and have a meal when we heard rifle shots. Raevsky sent someone to find out what was happening. They reported to him that the Turks had initiated crossfire on our foremost picket lines. I rode out with Semichev to have a look, since this was something completely new to me. We met a wounded Cossack: he was swaying in his saddle, all pale and bloody. Two Cossacks were supporting him. "Are there many Turks there?" Semichev asked. —"Flocking like swine, your Excellency," one of them answered. Just as we had passed through the ravine we suddenly saw on the slope of the opposite mountain as many as two hundred Cossacks mounted and lined up in loose order, and above them about five hundred Turks. The Cossacks were slowly retreating; the Turks were attacking with increasing boldness, they would take aim at about twenty paces and when they had fired would gallop back to their lines. Their high turbans, beautiful dolmans and glittering trappings of their horses were in sharp contrast with the blue uniforms and simple harness of the Cossacks. About fifteen of our men were already wounded. Lieutenant-Colonel Basov had sent for assistance. At the time he himself was wounded in the leg. The Cossacks were on the verge of panic. But Basov got back on his horse and remained in command. The reinforcements arrived in time. The Turks caught sight of them and disappeared at once, leaving behind them on the mountain the naked corpse of a Cossack, who had been decapitated and hacked to pieces. The Turks send severed heads to Constantinople, but the hands they dip in blood and then leave their imprint on their banners. The shooting quieted down. Eagles, ever the companions of troops, hovered above the mountain, seeking out their prey from on high. At this point a crowd of generals and officers appeared: Count Paskevich arrived and set out up the mountain behind which the Turks had disappeared. They were reinforced by 4,000 cavalry hidden in the depression and the gorges. From the height of the mountain the Turkish camp opened up before us, separated from us by gorges and hills. We got back late. As we rode through our camp I saw our wounded, five of whom died either that night or the next day. In the evening I paid a visit to young Osten-Saken, who had been wounded that very day in another skirmish.

Camp life was very much to my liking. The cannon got us up at sunrise. Sleep in a tent is surprisingly sound. At dinner we washed down Asian shishkebab with English beer and champagne chilled in the Tauris snows. Our company was varied. The beks of the Moslem regiments gathered in General Paskevich's tent; and conversation was conducted through an interpreter. In our army there were also people from our own Transcaucasian territories, as well as some inhabitants from regions that had recently been annexed. Among the latter I was particularly curious about the Yezidis, who are reputed in the Orient to be Devil worshippers. There are about three hundred families who live at the foot of Mount Ararat. They have recognized the rule of the Russian sovereign. Their chief, a tall, ugly man in a red tunic and black cap, would sometimes come bowing to General Raevsky, chief of all the cavalry. I tried to find out from the Yezidi the truth about their religion. To my questions he answered that the rumor that the Yezidis worship Satan was pure fiction; that they believe in the one God; that it is true that according to their law to damn the Devil is considered improper and base for he is now an unfortunate, but with time it is possible that he can be forgiven, since one must not set limits on the mercy of Allah. This explanation set my mind at rest. I was very happy for the Yezidis that they do not worship Satan; and their errors seemed to me already much more pardonable.

My man appeared in camp three days after me. He arrived together with a transport which in full view of the enemy had joined up safely with our army. NB: during the whole campaign not one cart from our numerous convoy was seized by the enemy. The orderliness with which the convoy followed the troops was indeed amazing.

In the morning of the seventeenth of June we heard firing again, and two hours later caught sight of the Karabakh Regiment returning with eight Turkish banners: Colonel Frideriks had been dealing with the enemy, which was ensconced behind stone obstructions, forced them out and drove them away; Osman-Pasha, who was in command of the cavalry, barely managed to save himself.

On the eighteenth of June the camp transferred to another location. On the nineteenth the cannon had hardly awakened us when the whole camp was in commotion. The generals went to their posts. The regiments lined up; the officers placed themselves with their platoons. I was left alone, not knowing in which direction to go, and left the horse to God's will. I met General Burtsov, who summoned me to the left flank. What's the left flank? I thought and continued on. I caught sight of General Muravyov, who had been positioning the cannon. Soon afterward the Turkish cavalry soldiers appeared and began circling about in the valley, engaging in an exchange of fire with our Cossacks. Meanwhile a thick crowd of their infantry was proceeding along the depression. General Muravyov gave orders to fire. The case-shot struck in the very center of the crowd. The Turks flocked to the side and hid behind an elevation. I saw Count Paskevich surrounded by his staff. The Turks were circling past our troops, which were separated from them by a deep gorge. The Count sent Pushchin to inspect the gorge. Pushchin galloped off. The Turks took him for a raider and fired a volley at him. Everybody burst out laughing. The Count gave orders to expose the cannon and fire. The enemy scattered over the mountain and in the depression. On the left flank, where Burtsov had summoned me, heated fighting was going on. Right in front of us (opposite the center) the Turkish cavalry was galloping. The Count sent General Raevsky against it, who led his Nizhegorod Regiment into the attack. The Turks disappeared. Our Tartars surrounded their wounded and swiftly stripped them, leaving them naked in the middle of the field. General Raevsky stopped at the edge of the gorge. Two squadrons, which had separated from the regiment, went too far in their pursuit; they were rescued by Colonel Simonich.

The battle quieted down; while we looked on the Turks began digging and hauling rocks to fortify their position in their usual way. They were left alone. We dismounted and began to make a meal on whatever was at hand. At this time some prisoners were brought to the Count. One of them was wounded brutally. They were questioned. About five o'clock the troops again received an order to march against the enemy. The Turks began to stir behind their barricades, received us with cannon shots, and began to retreat soon afterward. Our cavalry was in the front; we began to descend into the gorge; the ground kept breaking loose and rolling away under the horses' feet. My horse was in danger of falling at any moment, and in that case the Combined Ulan Regiment would have crossed right over me. But God saw me through. We had hardly got out on the wide road that goes through mountains when our whole cavalry began to gallop at full speed. The Turks were in flight; the Cossacks struck at the cannon which were abandoned along the road with their whips, and flew past. The Turks were rushing into the gorges on either side of the road; they had stopped firing—at least, not one bullet whistled past my ears. The first in the pursuit were our Tartar regiments, whose horses are distinguished by their speed and stamina. Biting at the bridle, my horse kept right after them; I could hardly hold her back. She stopped before the corpse of a young Turk which was lying across the road. He was about eighteen, I think; his pale girlish face had not been disfigured. His turban·was lying in the dust; the nape of his neck, which was shaved clean, had been pierced by a bullet. I slowed down to a walk; soon Raevsky caught up with me. In pencil on a scrap of paper he jotted down his report to Count Paskevich on the complete defeat of the enemy and rode on. I followed after him at a distance. Night fell. My tired horse was lagging behind and stumbling at every step. Count Paskevich gave orders not to stop the pursuit and was himself directing it. Our cavalry detachments overtook me; I saw Colonel Polyakov, the chief of the Cossack artillery which had played an important role that day, and arrived together with him at an abandoned settlement where Count Paskevich had stopped after ending the pursuit because of nightfall.

We found the Count in front of a fire on the roof of an underground saklya. The

prisoners were being brought to him. He was
questioning them. Almost all of the leaders
were also there. The Cossacks were holding
their horses by the reins. The fire lit up the
whole scene, which was worthy of Salvatore-
Roza; one could hear the brook in the darkness. At this point the Count received a
report that powder stores had been con-
cealed in the village and that there was
reason to fear an explosion. The Count left
the saklya with his entire entourage. We set
out toward our camp which was by now
thirteen versts from the spot where we had
spent the night. The road was full of cavalry
detachments. No sooner had we arrived than
suddenly the sky was lit up as by a meteor,
and we heard the hollow thud of an explosion.
The saklya which we had left only a quarter
of an hour before had exploded in the air: it
was there that the powder stores had been con-
cealed. The shower of rocks crushed several
Cossacks.

This is all that I managed to see at that
time. In the evening I found out that in this
battle they had defeated the Seraskir of
Arzrum who was on his way to joining Gaki-
Pasha with 30,000 troops. The Seraskir fled
to Arzrum; his troops which were scattered
behind Sagan-Lu were routed, the artillery
was taken, and Gaki-Pasha alone remained in
our power. Count Paskevich did not give him
time to regain control of the situation.

Chapter Four

The Battle with Gaki-Pasha. The Death of a Tartar Bek. The Hermaphrodite. The Captive Pasha. Araks. Shepherd's Bridge. Hassan Kale. A Hot Spring. The March to Arzrum. The Negotiations. The Taking of Arzrum. The Turkish Captives. The Dervish.

Next day the camp woke up before five and received an order to move out. When I had come out of my tent, I met Count Paskevich, who had risen before everyone else. He saw me. *"Êtes-vous fatigué de la journée d'hier?"—"Mais un peu, Mr le Comte."—"J'en suis fâché pour vous, car nous allons faire encore une marche pour joindre le Pacha, et puis il faudra poursuivre l'ennemi encore une trentaine de verstes."*

We were off—and toward eight o'clock we had come to a height from which Gaki-Pasha's camp was clearly visible. The Turks opened harmless fire from all their batteries. Meanwhile great commotion was noticeable in their camp. Weariness and the morning heat forced many of us to dismount and lie down on the fresh grass. I wound the reins around my hands and fell into a sweet sleep while waiting for the order to march. In a quarter of an hour I was awakened. Everything was on the move. On one side columns were advancing against the Turkish camp; on the other the cavalry was preparing to pursue the enemy. I was about to go after the Nizhegorod Regiment, but my horse was limping. I lagged behind. The Ulan Regiment rushed past me. Then Volkhovsky galloped by with three cannon. I found myself alone in the wooded mountains. I happened to meet a dragoon who reported that the forest was filled with the enemy. I turned back. I met General Muravyov with an infantry regiment. He had detached one company to the forest in order to clear it. As I approached the depression, I saw an extraordinary scene. Under a tree lay one of our Tartar beks, mortally wounded. Beside him his favorite was sobbing. A mullah, on his knees, was citing prayers. The dying bek was extremely calm and looked fixedly at his young friend. About five hundred prisoners had been gathered in the depression. Some wounded Turks were beckoning to me with signs, they probably took me for a doctor, and were begging for help which I could not give them. A Turk emerged from the forest, clutching his wound with a bloody rag. Some soldiers went up to him with the intention of finishing him off, perhaps out of humaneness. But this was more than I could endure; I interceded for the poor Turk and with difficulty brought him, exhausted and bleeding profusely, to his small group of comrades. With them was Colonel Anrep. He was smoking in a friendly fashion from their pipes, despite the fact that there were rumors that the plague had broken out in the Turkish camp. The prisoners were sitting, quietly conversing among themselves. Almost all were young. We rested and set out again. Bodies lay scattered all along the way. After about fifteen versts, I found the Nizhegorod Regiment, which had stopped on the bank of a stream running between the cliffs. The pursuit continued for several hours more. Toward evening we arrived in a valley surrounded by thick forest, and at last I could sleep as much as I wanted, after having covered more than eighty versts in those two days.

The next day the troops which had been pursuing the enemy received an order to return to camp. Then we learnt that there was a hermaphrodite among the prisoners. Raevsky, on my request, gave orders that he be brought in. I saw a tall rather heavy peasant with the face of an old snub-nosed Finnish woman. We examined him in the presence of a doctor. *Erat vir, mammosus ut femina, habebat t. non evolutos, p. que parvum et puerilem. Quaerebamus, sit ne exsectus?—Deus, respondit, castravit me.* This disease, known to Hippocrates, is according to testimony of travelers often encountered among the nomadic Tartars and the Turks. *Xoss* is the Turkish name for these purported hermaphrodites.

Our troops were quartered in the Turkish camp taken the day before. Count Paskevich's tent stood near the sprawling green tent of Gaki-Pasha, who had been taken prisoner by our Cossacks. I went to see him and found him surrounded by our officers. He was sitting crosslegged and smoking a pipe. He seemed to be about forty. Dignity and profound calm showed on his handsome face. When he was taken prisoner, he asked that he be given a cup of coffee and spared all questioning.

We were quartered in a valley. The snowy and wooded mountains of Sagan-Lu were now behind us. We advanced, no longer encountering the enemy at any point. The settlements were empty. The surrounding country is sad. We caught sight of the Araks river swiftly flowing between its stony banks. Fifteen versts from Hassan-Kale there is a bridge which is built beautifully and daringly on seven uneven arches. Legend attributes its construction to a shepherd who had grown rich and died a hermit on the summit of a hill, where to this day they show his grave, shaded by two solitary pines. The neighboring villagers come streaming to it to pay their respects. The bridge is called Chaban-Kepri (Shepherd's Bridge). The road to Tebriz lies across it.

A few paces from the bridge I visited the dark ruins of a caravan-sarai. I found no one in it except an ailing donkey which had probably been left there by the fleeing villagers.

In the morning of the twenty-fourth of June we set out for Hassan Kale, an ancient fortress, which had been taken the day before by Prince Bekovich. It was fifteen versts from the place where we had spent the night. The long marches had exhausted me. I was hoping to rest; but things turned out differently.

Before the departure of the cavalry some Armenians who lived in the mountains appeared in our camp demanding protection from the Turks, who three days before had driven away their cattle. Colonel Anrep, who had not made out very well what they wanted, imagined that a Turkish detachment was in the mountains and with one squadron of the Ulan Regiment galloped in that direction, leaving word for Raevsky that 3,000 Turks were in the mountains. Raevsky set out after him, in order to reinforce him in case of danger. I considered myself attached to the Nizhegorod Regiment, and galloped off to participate in the liberation of the Armenians greatly annoyed. When we had covered about twenty versts we rode into a village and saw several ulans, separated from their regiment, who hurriedly, with bared sabres, were pursuing several chickens. There one of the settlers explained to Raevsky that it was all a matter of 3,000 oxen which three days before had been driven away by the Turks and which it would be extremely easy to catch up with in two days or so. Raevsky ordered the ulans to discontinue their pursuit of the chickens and sent Colonel Anrep an order to return. We rode back, and when we had emerged from the mountains we arrived at Hassan Kale. But in that way we spent forty versts on a detour in order to save the life of some Armenian chickens, which did not seem at all amusing to me.

Hassan-Kale is considered the key to Arzrum. The city is built at the foot of a cliff crowned with a fortress. In it there were as many as a hundred Armenian families. Our camp stood in the wide plain which spreads before the fortress. There I visited a circular stone structure in which there is a hot iron-sulphurous spring.

The round pool is about six meters in diameter. I swam across it twice and suddenly felt dizziness and nausea, and had hardly enough strength to come out onto the stone edge of the spring. These baths are renowned in the Orient, but since they have no decent doctors there the inhabitants use them at random and probably without great success.

Under the walls of Hassan-Kale flows the little river Murts; its banks are covered with ferrous springs which well out from under the stones and flow into the river. They do not have as pleasant a flavor as the Caucasian Narzan but taste of copper.

On the twenty-fifth of June, the birthday of our Sovereign Emperor, the regiments heard a public prayer in our camp under the walls of the fortress. At dinner with Count Paskevich, when we were drinking the Sovereign's health, the Count announced the march to Arzrum. At five that afternoon the troops had already set out.

On the twenty-sixth of June we stopped in the mountains five versts from Arzrum. These mountains are called Ak-Dag (the white mountains); they are limestone. Our eyes smarted from the white, burning dust; the dreary landscape made one depressed. The proximity of Arzrum and the certainty of an end to the campaign comforted us.

In the evening Count Paskevich rode about to inspect the terrain. Turkish raiders who had been circling in front of our picket lines all day began to shoot at him. The Count threatened them a few times with his whip, without interrupting his discussion with General Muravyov. Their shots were left unanswered.

Meanwhile in Arzrum great confusion was taking place. The Seraskir, who had taken refuge in the city after his defeat, had spread a rumor about the complete rout of the Russians. And after him, the released prisoners had delivered Count Paskevich's appeal to the inhabitants. The refugees exposed the Seraskir's lie. Soon after they learnt about the rapid approach of the Russians. The people began to talk of surrender. The Seraskir and the troops were planning to defend themselves. Mutiny broke out. Some Franks were killed by the embittered mob.

Deputies from the people and the Seraskir appeared at our camp (in the morning of the twenty-sixth); the day went by in negotiations; at five in the afternoon the deputies set out for Arzrum, and with them General Prince Bekovich, who knew Asian languages and habits well.

The next morning our troops moved forward. On the eastern side of Arzrum, on the height of Top-Dag, was a Turkish battery. The regiments set out for it, answering the Turkish fire with drumbeat and music. The Turks fled, and Top-Dag was taken. I went there with the poet Yuzefovich. At the abandoned battery we found Count Paskevich with his entire entourage. From the height of the mountain, down in a depression, Arzrum opened up before us with its citadel, with its minarets, with its green roofs affixed one to the other. The Count was on horseback. Before him on the ground sat the

Turkish deputies, who had come with the keys to the city. But in Arzrum commotion was noticeable. Suddenly fire flashed on the city rampart, there was smoke, and round shots flew toward Top-Dag. Some of them swept past over Count Paskevich's head; *"Voyez les Turcs,"* he said to me, *"on ne peut jamais se fier à eux."* At this minute Prince Bekovich, who had been in Arzrum on negotiations since the day before, galloped up to Top-Dag. He reported that the Seraskir and the people had long since agreed to surrender, but, that some unruly Arnautians under the leadership of Topcha-Pasha had taken control of the city batteries and were rebelling. The generals rode up to the Count asking permission to silence the Turkish batteries. The dignitaries of Arzrum who found themselves under fire of their own cannon repeated the same request. The Count hesitated some time; finally he gave the order, saying: "That's enough of their foolishness." At once they brought up the cannon and began to fire, and the enemy barrage died away little by little. Our regiments set out for Arzrum, and on the 27th of June on the anniversary of the Battle of Poltava at six o'clock in the evening the Russian banner was unfolded over the citadel of Arzrum.

Raevsky set out for the city—I went with him; we rode into the city, which presented an astounding picture. From their flat roofs the Turks were looking at us sullenly. Armenians were thronging noisily in the narrow streets. Their little boys ran in front of our horses, crossing themselves and repeating: Christians! Christians!.. We rode up to the fortress where our artillery was entering; with extreme amazement I met my Artemy there, already riding around in the city despite the strict order that nobody from the camp should be absent without special permission.

The streets of the city are narrow and crooked. The houses are rather high. There are làrge numbers of people—the shops were locked. After spending about two hours in the city, I returned to camp: the Seraskir and the four Pashas who had been taken prisoners were already here. One of the Pashas, a wizened old man, a terrible bustler, was speaking vivaciously with our generals. When he saw me in my tail coat he asked who I was. Pushchin gave me the title of poet. The Pasha crossed his arms on his breast and bowed to me, saying through an interpreter: "Blessed be the hour when we meet a poet. The poet is brother to the dervish. He has neither a fatherland, nor earthly blessings; and while we, poor ones, worry about glory, about power, about treasures, he stands equal with the rulers of the earth and they bow to him."

Chapter Four

The Pasha's Oriental greeting pleased us all very much. I went to have a look at the Seraskir. On entering his tent I met his favorite page, a dark-eyed boy of about fourteen wearing rich Arnautian clothes. The Seraskir, a grayhaired old man of the most ordinary appearance, was sitting in deep despondency. Around him was a crowd of our officers. As I came out of his tent I saw a young man, half naked, in a sheepskin cap, with a club in his hand and a wineskin *(outre)* over his shoulders. He was shouting at the top of his voice. I was told that this was my brother, the dervish, who had come to greet the victors. They had a difficult time driving him away.

Pushkin, self-portrait, 1829

Chapter Five

Arzrum (incorrectly called Arzerum, Erz-
rum, Erzron) was founded about 415, during
Theodosius the Second, and called Theo-
dosiopolis. No historic associations are linked
with its name. All I knew about it was that it
was here, according to the testimony of Hadji-
Baba, that the Persian ambassador was given,
in reparation for some insult, calves' ears
rather than human ones.

Arzrum is considered the chief city of
Asian Turkey. It has been estimated that it
has as many as 100,000 inhabitants, but I
think this figure is exaggerated. Its houses
are made of stone, the roofs covered with
turf, which gives the city an extremely strange
appearance if you look at it from above.

The main land-route for trade between
Europe and the Orient goes through Arzrum.
But few goods are sold there; they are not
put out for sale, a fact which had also

been observed by Tournefort when he wrote
that a sick person might die in Arzrum from
the impossibility of procuring a spoonful of
rhubarb, while whole sackfuls of it were stored
in the city.

I know of no expression more nonsensi-
cal than the words: Asian luxury. This phrase
probably originated during the Crusades when
poor knights leaving the bare walls and oak
chairs of their castles had their first glimpse
of red divans, many-colored rugs, and daggers with colored gems on their hilts. Nowadays one can say: Asian poverty, Asian
swinishness, etc., but luxury is, of course, an
attribute of Europe. In Arzrum you cannot
buy for any money what you can find in a
general store in any district town of Pskov
Province.

The Arzrum climate is severe. The city
is built in a depression, which rises 7,000
feet above sea level. The mountains surrounding it are covered with snow the greater part
of the year. The land is unwooded but fertile.
It is watered by a large number of springs and
intersected at many points by aqueducts.
Arzrum is famed for its water. The Euphrates
flows three versts from the city. But there is
an abundance of fountains everywhere. At
each one there hangs a tin ladle on a chain,
and the good Moslems drink the water and
cannot praise it sufficiently.   Lumber is

supplied from Sagan-Lu.

In the Arzrum arsenal we found a large number of ancient weapons, helmets, coats of mail, sabres that had been rusting probably ever since the days of Godfrey. The mosques are low and dark. The cemetery is outside of the city. The tombstones are usually columns topped with stone turbans. The graves of two or three pashas are distinguished by greater intricacy, but there is nothing beautiful about them: no taste, no imagination... One traveler writes that of all Asian cities only in Arzrum did he find a tower clock, and it was not working.

The innovations devised by the Sultan have not yet penetrated as far as Arzrum. The troops still wear their picturesque oriental attire. A rivalry exists between Arzrum and Constantinople similar to that between Kazan and Moscow. Here is the beginning of a satirical poem composed by the janissary Amin-Oglu.

> *Now do the giaours extol Stambul,*
> *But tomorrow they will crush it,*
> *With iron heel, as they would a sleeping serpent,*
> *And they shall depart—and leave it so.*
> *Stambul slumbers as disaster comes.*
>
> *Stambul has renounced the prophet;*
> *There the cunning West has obscured*
> *The truth of the ancient East.*
> *For the sweetness of vice*

A Journey to Arzrum

Stambul has betrayed prayer and sabre.
Stambul no longer knows the sweat of battle
And drinks wine during the hour of prayer.

There the pure ardor of faith is dead.
There wives stalk the cemeteries,
They send old women to the crossroads,
And they bring men into the harems,
And the bribed eunuch sleeps.

But in mountainous Arzrum it is not so,
In our Arzrum of the many roads;
We do not sleep in shameful luxury,
We do not dip an unruly goblet into wine
To ladle out debauchery, fire and fury.

We fast: with sober flow
The holy waters slake our thirst:
A dauntless and mettlesome host,
Our skillful horsemen fly into battle.

Our harems are impenetrable,
The eunuchs strict, they cannot be bought,
And the wives meekly dwell therein.

I lived in the Seraskir's palace in the rooms where the harem had been. A whole day I wandered through countless passages, from room to room, from roof to roof, from staircase to staircase. The palace looked as though it had been plundered; the Seraskir as he planned his escape, took whatever he could with him. The divans were in tatters, the rugs had been removed. As I walked around in the city the Turks would beckon to me and show me their tongues. (They take every Frank for a doctor). I soon grew tired of this and was ready to answer in kind. The evenings I spent with the clever and affable Sukhorukov; the similarity of our occupations brought us together. He spoke to me of his literary intentions, of his historical research which he had once undertaken with such zeal and skill. The modest nature of his desires and demands is in truth quite touching. What a pity it will be if they are not fulfilled.

The Seraskir's palace presented a picture of constant animation: where the sullen pasha used to smoke silently among his wives and shameless boys, his vanquisher was receiving reports on the victories of his generals, distributing pashalics, and discussing new novels. The Pasha of Mush came to Count Paskevich to ask him to be given his nephew's position. As he walked through the palace the solemn Turk stopped in one of the rooms, uttered a few words with great animation, and then fell into deep thought: in this very room his father had been beheaded at the command of the Seraskir. These are genuine impressions of the Orient! The wonderful Bey-bulat, the terror of the Caucasus, came to Arzrum with two headmen from the Circassian villages which had rebelled during the last wars. They dined with Count Paskevich.

Bey-bulat, a man of about thirty-five, is undersized and broadshouldered. He does not speak Russian, or pretends that he does not. His arrival in Arzrum made me very happy: he had already been my guarantee in the safe crossing through the mountains and Kabarda.

Osman-Pasha, who was captured near Arzrum and sent to Tiflis along with the Seraskir, requested Count Paskevich to insure the safety of the harem that he had left in Arzrum. During the first days we almost forgot about it. Once at dinner, while discussing the silence of this Moslem city, occupied by 10,000 troops and in which not one of the inhabitants had even once complained of violence on the part of our soldiers, the Count recalled Osman-Pasha's harem and ordered Mr. A***** to go over to the Pasha's house and ask his wives if they were content and whether or not they had been offended in any way. I asked permission to accompany Mr. A*****. We set out. Mr. A***** took along as interpreter a Russian officer whose story is curious. At eighteen he had been taken prisoner by the Persians. They emasculated him, and for more than twenty years he served as a eunuch in the harem of one of the sons of the Shah. He told us about his misfortune and about his stay in Persia with touching openheartedness. In a physiological sense his testimony was precious.

We arrived at Osman-Pasha's house; we were led into an open room, decorated very decently, even with taste—on the stained-glass windows there were inscriptions taken from the Koran. One of them seemed to me very ingenious for a Moslem harem: *it behooves you to bind and loose.* We were brought coffee in little cups trimmed with silver. An old man with a venerable white beard, Osman-Pasha's father, came in the name of the wives to thank Count Paskevich, but Mr. A***** said flatly that he had been sent to Osman-Pasha's wives and wanted to see them in order to ascertain from them personally that they had nothing to complain of during the absence of their husband. Hardly had the Persian prisoner managed to translate all this when the old man, to show his indignation, began to click his tongue and announced that he absolutely could not accede to our demand, and that if the Pasha upon his return were to find out that outsiders had seen his wives, he, the old man, as well as all the harem servants, would have their heads chopped off. The attendants, among whom there was not one eunuch, corroborated the old man's words, but Mr. A***** was firm. "You fear your Pasha," he told them, "and I my Seraskir, and I dare not disobey his orders." There was nothing else to be done.We were led through a garden where two meager fountains were spouting. We approached a small stone structure. The old man placed himself between us and the door, opened it cautiously without letting the bolt out of his hands, and we saw a woman, covered from head to yellow slippers by a white yashmak. Our interpreter repeated his question to her: we heard the clucking of a seventy-year-old woman; Mr. A***** interrupted her. "This is the Pasha's mother," he said, "but I was sent to his wives, bring one of them here"; they were all amazed at the giaours' shrewdness: the old woman went away and returned in a minute with a woman covered in the same way as she— from under the veil one heard a gentle voice, young and pleasant. She thanked the Count for his kindness to the poor widows and praised the manners of the Russians. Mr. Abramovich managed skillfully to engage her in further conversation. Meanwhile, as I looked about me, I suddenly saw just above the door a small round window, and in this round window five or six round heads with black inquisitive eyes. I was about to communicate my discovery to Mr. A*****, but the little heads started shaking and winking, and several little fingers began to threaten me, to let me know that I should keep silent. I did as I was bid and did not share my discovery. They were all pleasant to look at, but there was not a single beauty; the one at the door, conversing with Mr. A*****, was probably the Sovereign of the harem, the treasury of hearts—the Rose of love—at least, that is what I imagined.

At last Mr. A***** concluded his questioning. The door was closed. The faces in the little window disappeared. We inspected the garden and the house and returned quite pleased with our mission.

It was in this way that I got to see a harem: very few Europeans have managed to do this. There you have the beginning for an Oriental novel.

The war seemed to be over. I began to prepare for the return trip. On the fourteenth of July I went to the public baths and was not very happy with life. I cursed the filth of the linen, the vile service, etc. How can one compare the baths in Arzrum with those in Tiflis!

As I returned to the palace I learned from Konovnitsyn, who was standing guard, that the plague had broken out in Arzrum. I immediately reflected on all the horrors of a quarantine and that very day I decided to leave. When one has had no experience of it the idea that one is in the presence of the plague can be very unpleasant. In the hope of ridding myself of this reaction, I set out for a walk around the bazaar. I stopped in front of a weapon shop, and began examining a dagger when suddenly someone tapped me on the shoulder. I looked around: behind me stood a horrible beggar. He was as pale as death; from his red festered eyes tears were streaming. The thought of the plague again flashed in my mind. I pushed the beggar away with a feeling of repugnance that is impossible to describe and returned home very displeased with my outing.

Curiosity, however, got the upper hand; the next day I accompanied the doctor to the camp where those infected with the plague were kept. I did not dismount and took the precaution to stand with the wind behind me. A sick man was led out to us from a tent; he was extremely pale and staggered as though he were drunk. Another infected man was lying there unconscious. When I had examined the plague-stricken man, and promised the poor unfortunate a speedy recovery, I turned my attention to the two Turks who led him by the arm, undressed and touched him as though the plague were nothing more than a head cold. I confess, I was ashamed of my European timidity in the presence of such equanimity and hastened back to the city.

On the nineteenth of July when I came to take my leave of Count Paskevich I found him in intense grief. He had received the sad news that General Burtsov had been killed at Baiburt. He was sorry for brave Burtsov, but this incident could as well prove disastrous for the whole of our undermanned army, which had penetrated so deeply into foreign territory and was surrounded by hostile populations that were ready to rebel at the rumor of the first defeat. And so the war recommenced! The Count proposed that I witness the subsequent engagements. But I was in a hurry to get back to Russia... The Count presented me with a Turkish sabre as a memento. I have kept it in remembrance of my travels hard on the footsteps of that brilliant hero through the conquered wilderness of Armenia. That very day I left Arzrum.

I journeyed back to Tiflis along the route which was already familiar to me. Places which had only recently been made alive by the presence of 15,000 troops were silent and sad. I crossed Sagan-Lu and could hardly recognize the place where our camp had stood. In Gumry I had to endure a three-day quarantine. I saw Bezobdal once again and left the lofty plains of cold Armenia for sultry Georgia. I arrived in Tiflis on the first of August. I remained there for a few days in amiable and happy company. A few evenings were spent in the gardens listening to music and Georgian songs. I continued on my way. My crossing over the mountains was noteworthy from the

fact that near Kobi a storm overtook me
during the night. In the morning as I rode past
Kazbek I saw a wonderful spectacle. White,
torn clouds were stretching across the summit of the mountain and a lone monastery,
bathed in the rays of the sun, seemed to be
floating in the air, borne on the clouds. The
Furious Gorge also showed itself to me in all
its grandeur: the ravine, which had swollen
with the rain, surpassed in its ferocity the
Terek itself, which was also roaring furiously
nearby. The banks had been mangled; enormous boulders had been uprooted and were
obstructing the stream. A great number of
Ossets were working on the road. I made the
crossing safely. At last I rode out of the
narrow ravine into the expanse of the wide
plains of Great Kabarda. In Vladikavkaz I
found Dorokhov and Pushchin. Both were
on their way to spas to be treated for the
wounds they had received in the current
campaigns. On a table at Pushchin's I found
some Russian magazines. The first article that
I came across was an analysis of one of my
compositions. In it I and my verses were
abused in every possible way. I began to read
it aloud. Pushchin stopped me, demanding
that I read it with greater mimetic artistry. It
should be pointed out that the analysis was
adorned with the usual devices of our criticism:
it consisted of a discussion between a deacon,

a maker of communion bread, and a proof-reader, who was the Zdravomysl of this little comedy. Pushchin's suggestion struck me as so amusing that the vexation which reading the article had produced in me completely disappeared and we burst out laughing in all sincerity.

Such was my first greeting in our beloved fatherland.

TRANSLATOR'S NOTES

Alexander Sergeevich Pushkin (May 26, 1799-January 29, 1837) published *A Journey to Arzrum (Puteshestvie v Arzrum)* in the first issue of his literary magazine the *Contemporary (Sovremennik)* in April 1836. It was based on actual experiences during a trip in the summer of 1829.

This translation, the first into English, is based on the "large" Academy edition (A. S. Pushkin, *Polnoe sobranie sochinenii,* t. VIII, kn. 1 [AN SSSR, 1940], 443-483). While the translation stays very close to most features of the text, where Pushkin circumspectly gives only initials (Count P., R., etc.) the full names (Count Pushkin, Raevsky) are always given in the translation. All dates are given in Old Style; in the nineteenth century dates are therefore twelve days behind the Gregorian calendar.

Translations of all non-Russian passages which occur in Pushkin's text are included in the notes which follow.

PREFACE

Page 11

Voyages en Orient... - *Journeys to the Orient Undertaken by Order of the French Government. (French.)* This was Victor Fontanier's second journey to Anatolia, published in Paris.

The campaign of 1829 - The war between Russia and Turkey of 1828-29 was conducted on two fronts: in the Balkans, and in eastern Turkey. The Russian army was under the command of Field Marshals Ivan Ivanovich Dibich-Zabalkansky ("who went across to the Balkans") [1785-1831] and Ivan Fedorovich Paskevich-Erivansky ("of Erivan' ") [1782-1856].

Un poète distingué... - A poet, distinguished by his imagination, found in so many lofty deeds of which he was the witness not the subject for a narrative poem, but for a satire. *(French.)*

Alexei Stepanovich Khomyakov (1804-60), writer, historian. In 1830 he published some poems concerning his recent stay in Adrianople, the city in the Balkans.

Andrei Nikolaevich Muravyov (1806-74), writer on religious themes. His *A Journey to the Holy Land (Puteshestvie ko sviatym mestam)* was published in 1832.

The Detached Caucasus Corps was at this time (1829) largely made up of former Decembrists, i.e., participants in the officers' rebellion of December 14, 1825, and their sympathizers.

Parmi les chefs... - Among the leaders who commanded it (Prince Paskewitch's army) one could distinguish General Mouravief... Prince Tsitsevaze of Georgia... Prince Beboutof of Armenia... Prince Potemkine, General Raiewsky, and finally—M. Pouchkine... who had left the capital in order to sing the praises of his compatriot's exploits. *(French.)*

Nikolai Nikolaevich Muravyov (1794-1866), Raevsky's immediate superior (see p. 12), called Karsky ("of Kars") after distinguishing himself at the taking of that city in June 1829.

Page 12

Tsitsevaze - This is a rendition of Chavchavadze, Alexander Garsevanovich (1786-1846), the prominent Georgian poet, Griboedov's father-in-law (see p. 17). Born in St. Petersburg, he served as an officer in the Russian army that entered Paris in 1814.

Vasily Osipovich Bebutov (1791-1858) took part in the Napoleonic wars and had been Ermolov's aide-de-camp (see p. 15).

Nikolai Nikolaevich Raevsky (1801-43), Commander of the Nizhegorod Regiment of Dragoons. He had been Pushkin's close friend since 1820.

("Nizhegorod" was an abbreviation of Nizhny Novgorod, the city on the Volga now called Gorky.)

Sagan-Lu - a mountain ridge in eastern Turkey.

Seraskir - The Commander-in-Chief, or minister of war, of the Turkish army. The name of this Seraskir was Salih Pasha.

Osman-Pasha - The title Pasha was one of honor, not hereditary, and always followed the name. It denoted the highest official of a province in Turkey.

Mr. Commercial Consul - Pushkin uses this title ironically. It was rumored that Fontanier was a spy for the French government.

Page 13

...all that I have written... - This was not quite true. Pushkin's journey had provided material for some travel notes, published under the title "The Georgian Military Highway" ("Voennaia gruzinskaia doroga") in 1830 in the *Literary Gazette (Literaturnaia gazeta),* and for several poems written in 1829, including "On the hills of Georgia..." ("Na kholmakh Gruzii..."), "To the Kalmyk Girl" ("Kalmychke"), "From Gafiz" ("Iz Gafiza"), "Oleg's Sword" ("Olegov shchit"), "The Caucasus" ("Kavkaz"), "The Avalanche" ("Obval"), "The Monastery on Mount Kazbek" ("Monastyr' na Kazbeke"), and "Turkish Cavalry Soldier" ("Delibash").

CHAPTER ONE

Page 15

The headlines for the five chapters do not exist in Pushkin's manuscripts. They first appear in the *Contemporary*.

Two hundred versts - About 133 miles. One verst equals 0.6629 miles.

Alexei Petrovich Ermolov (1772-1861) had been

the Commander-in-Chief of the Russian army in the Caucasus before Paskevich, of whom he was strongly critical. At the time of Pushkin's visit, Ermolov was officially in disgrace.

Page 16

George Dawe (1781-1829), English portrait painter, creator of The Military Gallery in the Winter Palace, St. Petersburg. Containing more than 400 portraits of Russian generals of the War of 1812, it also includes the portrait of Ermolov.

Circassian - Several people of the Caucasus region are mentioned in the *Journey*. The Circassians and Ossets were mountain tribes. The Nogais and Kalmyks were nomads living on the steppes just north of the Caucasus.

The Count of Erivan' - The Russian *Graf Erivansky* is close to what Ermolov insists on calling him, *Graf Erikhonsky* (Count of Jericho), referring to the Biblical legend of Joshua and the battle of Jericho (Joshua, VI). Throughout the work Paskevich is referred to with his title—"the Count." This is somewhat pointed, since it had been given him only in 1828, and he was well-known for his love of flattery.

Shumla - A fortress in the Balkans (now Bulgaria), which had not fallen to the Russians.

Count Tolstoy - Probably Fyodor Ivanovich Tolstoy (1782-1846), called "The American," because he had visited the Aleutian Islands, then part of Russian America. At this time he was serving as intermediary in the marriage negotiations between Pushkin and his future wife. —The writers Lev Nikolaevich Tolstoy (1828-1910) and Alexei Konstantinovich Tolstoy (1817-75) both belonged to this same branch of the Tolstoy family.

Karamzin's History - Nikolai Mikhailovich Karamzin (1766-1826), major writer and historian. His *History of the Russian State (Istoriia gosudarstva*

Rossiiskogo) was published in 1818-29.

Andrei Mikhailovich Kurbsky (1528-83), Prince, military leader, strong opponent of Ivan the Terrible.

Con amore - With love. *(Italian.)*

Page 17

Some German generals - This refers to Dibich, e.g., who was German-born but in Russian service.

Alexander Sergeevich Griboedov (1795-1829), diplomat and playwright. He was appointed ambassador to Persia in 1828. For more on Griboedov, see the narrator's own discussion in Chapter Two, pp. 46-48.

Griboedov's verse - It may be interesting to note that Ermolov, when describing this to the poet Davydov said that his jaws ached from chewing the verse, not reading it.

Odessa mud - Pushkin had spent part of his exile (1823-24) in this Black Sea port.

Vladimir Alexeevich Musin-Pushkin (1798-1854), son of the famous collector of manuscripts. He had been arrested in connection with the Decembrist rebellion but received only a light sentence of demotion.

Page 18

Herds of indomitable mares... - From "Peter the Great in Ostrogozhsk" ("Petr Velikyi v Ostrogozhske") in *Thoughts (Dumy,* 1823) by Kondraty Fedorovich Ryleev (1795-1826), poet, Decembrist. Ryleev was one of five hanged for their participation in the Decembrist rebellion, and his name was therefore not allowed to appear under this verse.

Alexander Osipovich Orlovsky (1777-1832), well-known Polish artist.

Page 19

Circe - Famous sorceress in Greek legend. Odysseus and his men visited her island and were changed into swine.

Stavropol - One of a line of Russian fortresses along the southern boundaries of the Empire, built in 1777.

Nine years before - While in exile in the South of Russia, Pushkin spent part of the summer of 1820 in the Caucasus with the Raevsky family.

Goryachie vody (Hot Springs) was also called *Kavkazskie mineral'nye vody* (The Caucasian Mineral Springs). The place Pushkin describes was later named Pyatigorsk.

Page 20

Alexander Nikolaevich Raevsky (1795-1868), the older of the brothers, for some time Pushkin's Byronic idol. He is said to have inspired Pushkin's poem "The Demon," which was written in 1823.

Vladikavkaz - Since 1931 Ordzhonikidze.

Brichka - A long open horse-drawn carriage with a folding top over the rear seat and a front seat facing it.

Page 21

Ivan Vasilievich Gudovich (1741-1820) had commanded the Russian troops in Dagestan and Georgia in three wars against Turkey: 1768-74, 1787-91, and 1806-1812.

Page 22

Aul - A Caucasian mountain village.
Mullah - A teacher of Islam, religious leader.

Page 23

Disarming the Crimean Tartars - The Crimea had been annexed by Catherine II in 1783.

Page 24

Our annexation - The east coast of the Black

Sea, conquered by Catherine II in 1783, was again declared Russian in the Treaty of Adrianople, September, 1829, which concluded the war between Russia and Turkey.

Mansur (means: victorious; real name: Ushurma) [died in 1794], a Circassian who in 1785 proclaimed a holy war for his faith, Islam. He was captured by the Russians in 1791 and imprisoned in the Schlüsselburg Fortress, where he died. That he died at the Solovetsky monastery was just a legend.

Page 25

Saklya - A small stone dwelling.

...like a warrior... - In English in the original. From "The Burial of Sir John Moore" (1817) by Charles Wolfe (1791-1823), an Irish poet. The poem, greatly admired by Byron, was popular in Russia through the translation of Ivan Kozlov (1779-1840).

Yashmak - The veil worn by Moslem women.

Page 26

Emil Stjernvall-Walleen (1806-90) was traveling to the Caucasus with his brother-in-law Count Musin-Pushkin (see p. 17). Stjernvall was Finnish, but lived and worked in St. Petersburg.

Imatra - A waterfall in Finland.

...the thundering river... - From Stanza 72 of "The Waterfall" ("Vodopad") by Gavrila Romanovich Derzhavin (1743-1816), major Russian poet.

Page 27

Fyodor Alexandrovich Bekovich - Cherkassky ("the Circassian") was actually Kabardinian by nationality. He came into Russian service in 1806. After the taking of Kars, he became the manager of the Pashalic of Kars.

Kakhetinsky wine - From a region in the Caucasus.

And in goatskins... - From the *Iliad,* Book III, after the Russian translation by Ermil Ivanovich Kostrov (about 1750-90). —A more recent translation of the *Iliad* had been made by Nikolai Ivanovich Gnedich (1784-1833), published in 1829.

The Prisoner of the Caucasus - Kavkazskii plennik was a long narrative poem published by Pushkin in 1822.

Turkish prisoners - These Turks were prisoners of war in the on-going military operations.

Page 28

My friend Sheremetev -Probably Peter Vasilievich Sheremetev (1799-1837) who had worked in the Russian Embassy in Paris. Pushkin met him in the Caucasus spas on the way back (August 1829).

One traveler - The traveler Pushkin cites here is "N...N..." whose anonymous work *Notes during a Trip to the Caucasus and Georgia in 1827 (Zapiski vo vremia poezdki na Kavkaz i v Gruziiu v 1827 godu)* was published in 1829. Pushkin owned this book and used it in reworking his travel notes ("The Georgian Military Highway") into *A Journey to Arzrum.*

The Abduction of Ganimed - This painting by Rembrandt is in the Dresden Art Gallery, and was popular in gravures. In Greek mythology Ganimed was a beautiful boy, whom Zeus abducted and made into a wine-waiter.

Queen Daria - Pushkin read about this legend in *Voyage dans la Russie meridionale et particulièrement dans les provinces situées au delà du Caucase fait depuis 1820 jusqu'en 1824 (Journey in South Russia and Especially in the Provinces Situated Beyond the Caucasus, Undertaken from 1820 to 1824)* by the French consul to Tiflis, J. F. Gamba (1763-1833). The book was published in Paris in 1826.

Darial - (Persian Dar-i-Alan) means "Gate of the Alans." This was the medieval name for the Ossets.

Pliny the Elder (Gaius Plinius Secundus; 23 or 24-79 A.D.), Roman historian and geographer, author of the celebrated *Historiae Naturalis XXXVII (Natural History in 37 Books)*.

Page 29

Diri odoris - "Of foul odor." *(Latin.)*

Count Potocki - Pushkin read the information from Pliny in *Voyage dans les steps d'Astrakhan et du Caucase (A Journey to the Steppes of Astrakhan and to the Caucasus),* published in Paris, 1829, by Jan Potocki (1761-1815), Polish count, historian, linguist, traveler, writer. His "Spanish novels" include *Manuscrit trouvé à Saragosse (A Manuscript Found in Saragossa,* 1814), also originally written in French.

Prince Kazbek - Probably Nikolai Gabrielevich Kazbek (Kazibeg), whose family had ruled this area for generations.

Chikhir' - Georgian red wine.

Page 30

Chatyrdag - Pushkin had sailed from Kefa (now Feodosia) to Yurzuf (now Gurzuf) westward along the southern shore of the Crimea, thus passing Mount Chatyrdag, with the Raevskys in the late summer of 1820.

...holds up the horizon... - From "Half-soldier" ("Polusoldat," 1826) by Denis Vasilievich Davydov (1784-1839), a minor poet.

The Persian Prince - Khozrev-Mirza (1812-78), grandson of Feth Ali Shah (1771-1834). He was on his way to St. Petersburg with official apologies for the massacre of the Russian mission in Teheran, January 30, 1829, in which Griboedov among others perished.

Fazil-Khan (died 1852), Persian poet, Khozrev-

Mirza's teacher. He decided to stay in Russia, and went to live and teach in Tiflis, where he also died. Pushkin wrote the following lines upon their meeting: "Both the day and the hour are blessed,/ When in the Caucasus mountains/ Fate brought us together" ("Blagosloven i den' i chas,/ Kogda v gorakh Kavkaza/ Sud'ba soedinila nas"). Cf., the Pasha's greeting in Chapter Four, p. 76.

Page 31

Boris Gavrilovich Chilyaev (real name: Babana Chiladze) [1798-1850], Georgian by nationality. From 1828 he was the ruler over the mountain tribes along the Georgian Military Highway. The rough draft of Pushkin's note asking for assistance has been preserved.

Nikolai Gavrilovich Ogarev - Supervisor of the repair work along the roads.

Page 32

A landslide - Pushkin got the information of the large landslide from Gamba (see p. 28), but supplied the year "1827" himself; Gamba has 1817.

Page 35

Abaz - An old Georgian coin, at the time worth about twenty kopeks in silver. The *abaz* got its name from Shah Abbas I (1587-1628), whose image was printed on Persian coins.

De la liberté grande - For taking such a great liberty. (*French.*)

Order for posthorses - This was the *podorozhnaia* necessary for travel in the Russian Empire.

Rinaldo-Rinaldini - A well-born robber, hero of the novel by the same name of Christian August Vulpius (1762-1827), a German writer.

The Roman campaigns - Those of Gnaeus

Pompeius Magnus (Pompey the Great; 106-48 B.C.), which in 65 B.C. led to Roman hegemony over Iberia, as Georgia was then called.

CHAPTER TWO

Page 37

Kishinev - Then a town in Bessarabia, now the capital of the Moldavian Soviet Socialist Republic. Pushkin had spent part of his exile here (1820).

Page 38

...a lovely Georgian maid... - In English in the original. Thomas Moore (1779-1852), Irish romantic poet. *Lalla Rookh* (1817) was a tremendous success with the public, but Pushkin was not generally fond of Moore's poetry. Moore actually has "...country maidens' looks" in line 3.

Page 39

E sempre bene - And that was all right. *(Italian.)*
Pavel Stepanovich Sankovsky (1798-1832), first editor of the first Russian newspaper in Transcaucasia. *The Tiflis Record,* founded in 1828, was published in three languages—Russian, Georgian, and Persian. Sankovsky mentioned Pushkin and his stay in the Caucasus several times in the paper.
Pavel Dmitrievich Tsitsianov (1754-1806), a previous Commander-in-Chief of Georgia.

Page 40

Aga-Mohammed (1742-97), Shah.
Alexander I (1777-1825), Emperor of Russia from 1801.
Lezginka - "A courtship dance of the Caucasus mountains in which the woman moves with graceful

ease while the man dances wildly about her."
(Webster)

Soul, recently born... - This romance by Dimitri
Iosifovich Tumanishvili (died 1821) was popular in
Tiflis during Pushkin's stay there. Working from a
literal translation, he adapted it to Russian.

Page 41

The unfortunate Clarence - George, Duke of
Clarence (1449-78), brother of Edward IV (1442-83),
King of England, who sentenced him to death for
treason. The rumor spread that he had been drowned
in a butt of malmsey wine.

Tbilis-Kalar - The Georgian name for Tiflis (now
Tbilisi) was *Tbilis-Kalak*, not *-Kalar*. This same mistake
can be found in Ioann-Anton Gul'denstedt's (1745-81)
*A Geographic and Statistical Description of Georgia
and the Caucasus (Geograficheskoe i statisticheskoe
opisanie Gruzii i Kavkaza,* 1809), which Pushkin may
have read.

Page 42

Nikolai Andreevich Samoylov (died 1842), officer in the Preobrazhensk Regiment, former adjutant
of Ermolov, first cousin of the Raevsky brothers and
sisters.

Young titular councilors - Akim Nikolaevich
Nakhimov (1782-1814), poetaster, has in his satire
"Cry out, bureaucrat..." ("Vosplach', kantseliarist...")
a line about the "coveted rank of assessor." A titular
councilor could rise on the scale to become assessor,
which was the lowest rank resulting in noble status.

Nikolai Martyanovich Sipyagin (1775-1828), military governor of Tiflis. He had died under mysterious circumstances.

Page 43

Stepan Stepanovich Strekalov (1782-1856) took

over as military governor of Tiflis when Sipyagin died, and served from 1828 to 1831. He had orders from Paskevich to keep Pushkin under secret surveillance.

Page 44

Burning nights!... - Compare with "Southern stars! Black eyes!/ Fires of an alien sky..." from a poem written in 1828 by Peter Andreevich Vyazemsky (1792-1878), poet, Pushkin's friend.

Page 46

"Griboed" means literally "mushroom-eater," which is the base for the playwright's name.

Vous ne connaissez pas... - You do not know those people: you shall see that it will be necessary to play with knives. *(French.)*

His mutilated corpse - An eyewitness account, published in *Blackwood's Magazine* (Edinburgh, Sept. 1830, pp. 502-12), says that the body of "Grebayedoff" was not mutilated.

Page 47

The Moscow Telegraph - A bi-weekly journal of science and literature, published 1825-34.

Woe from Wit (Gore ot uma) was written in 1823-24, published in 1833.

Page 48

N. A. Buturlin (1801-67), aide-de-camp of the military minister A. I. Chernyshev, was keeping Pushkin under surveillance.

Page 50

Mount Ararat cannot be seen from Gumry. The twin-peaked, snowcapped mountain near this place is called Aragats.

Page 52

Caravan-sarai - In the middle east, a public building for the shelter of caravans and other travelers.

Page 55

"To the Kalmyk Girl" ("Kalmychke"). This poem was printed in the *Literary Gazette* in July 1830 over the signature "Krs."

Tauris, Tavrida - Although usually meaning the Crimea, Tauris refers here widely to an area south of the Black Sea.

CHAPTER THREE

Page 57

Ivan Grigorievich Burtsov (1794-1829), arrested in 1826 for Decembrist sympathies, was for half a year confined in a fortress and then removed to the Caucasus. He was one of the most notable military talents in the war with Turkey.

The Nizhegorod Regiment of Dragoons together with the Ulan Regiment (see p. 64) made up the cavalry under the command of Raevsky.

Page 58

Vladimir Dmitrievich Volkhovsky (1798-1841), General. He had started in the Lycée with Pushkin in 1811, and was yet another old friend who had been sent to the Caucasus after the Decembrist rebellion.

Mikhail Ivanovich Pushchin (1800-69), brother of Pushkin's closest friend during the years in the Lycée, Ivan Pushchin (1798-1859). He had been sent to Siberia in 1826 and then to the Caucasus.

Heu! fugaces... - Ah! Postumus, Postumus, flying/ The years pass by... *(Latin.)* From Quintus Horatius Flaccus (Horace; 65-8 B.C.), *Odes:* Book II: XIV.

Page 59

...*nec Armeniis...* - ...and in Armenia,/ Friend
Valgius, the rigid ice does not stay/ The whole year
round... *(Latin.)* Also Horace, *Odes,* Book II: IX.

Nikolai Nikolaevich Semichev (1792-1830), par-
ticipant in the War of 1812. After the Decembrist rebellion he was sent to the Caucasus.

Page 60

P. T. Basov - In 1829 he commanded a Don
Cossack Regiment bearing his name.

Page 61

Young Osten-Saken - As distinct from his older
relative, the Commander of the Detached Caucasus
Corps.

Bek - A commander of Moslem troops in Transcaucasia.

The Yezidis - Pushkin had among his papers a
"Notice sur la secte des Yezidis"*(French.)*

Page 62

B. A. Frideriks (1797-1874) commanded the
Erivan Regiment of Carabiniers (light cavalry).

Page 64

I. O. Simonich (died 1850), Commander of the
Georgian Regiment of Grenadiers. He had fought on
the French side in the Napoleonic wars, and was captured in 1812. After the Peace of Paris (1814) he went
into Russian service.

The Combined Ulan Regiment (light cavalry)
was made up of people who had taken active part in
the Decembrist rebellion and was therefore designated
only by three asterisks (*** Ulan Regiment) when
the *Journey* was first published.

Salvatore Rosa (1615-73), Italian painter, poet, actor, musician. He was especially remembered for his romantic landscapes (with shepherds) and battle scenes, as well as his flamboyant personality.

CHAPTER FOUR

Page 67

"Êtes-vous fatigué..." - "Are you tired from yesterday?" —"Well, a little, Count." —"I'm sorry about that, for we must march again to catch up with the Pasha, and then we must pursue the enemy for another thirty versts or so." *(French.)*

Page 69

Roman Romanovich Anrep (died 1830), Commander of the Combined Ulan Regiment. He suffered from fits of madness. In the beginning of 1830 he wandered down into a swamp and died from exposure.

Erat vir... - This was a man with a woman's breasts, underdeveloped t[esticles], a small and boyish p[enis]. We asked whether he had been emasculated?—God, he answered, castrated me. *(Latin.)*

Page 72

Six meters - Actually, "three *sazhen'* "–about 6.5 meters. One *sazhen'* equals 2.134 m.

Page 73

Narzan - Strong mineral water from a spring by the same name in the Caucasus spas (Kislovodsk).

Page 74

Frank - A West European.
Mikhail Vladimir Yuzefovich (1802-89), poet

and archeologist. He shared a tent with Lev Sergeevich Pushkin (1805-52), the poet's brother; both were aides-de-camp of Raevsky. He left interesting reminiscences about Pushkin's stay at the front.

Page 75

"Voyez les Turcs..." - "Look at the Turks, ... one can never trust them." *(French.)*

The Battle of Poltava took place on June 27, 1709, during the Nordic War (1700-21) between Russia and Sweden. Russia won.

Page 76

Dervish - A Moslem monk.

Page 77

Outre - Wineskin. *(French.)*

CHAPTER FIVE

Page 79

Arzrum - In West European languages, this city has usually been rendered Erzerum or Erzurum.

Theodosius II (401-50), Emperor of East Rome (408-450).

Calves' ears - Approximate rendition of an episode from *The Adventures of Hadji Baba of Ispahan* by James J. Morier (1780-1849), an English diplomat. The novel was first published in Persian in 1824, then in English in 1828. Osip Senkovsky ("Baron Brambeus," 1800-58) published a free Russian translation in 1830.

Page 80

Joseph Pitton de Tournefort (1656-1708), French botanist. His book *Narrative of a Journey to the Occident (Relation d'un voyage du Levant),* out of which Pushkin is quoting (from the eighteenth letter), was published in 1718 in Amsterdam.

The Province of Pskov was situated between Lakes Pskov-Peipus (Chudskoe) and Ilmen, about 200 miles south of St. Petersburg. Mikhailovskoe, Pushkin's estate, where he spent part of the years 1824-26 in exile, is situated here.

Page 81

Godfrey (Godfred; Gottfried) of Bouillon (about 1060-1100), Duke of Lower Lorraine. He participated in the first crusade. His deeds were described by Torquato Tasso in *Gerusalemme liberata (Jerusalem Delivered,* 1575).

Innovations - The Sultan was Mahmud II (1785-1839), who in 1826 had reorganized the Turkish army by relinquishing the janissaries, the old elite corps of soldiers.

Now do the giaours... - The poem, purportedly by a certain Amin-Oglu, was written by Pushkin at Boldino in the fall of 1830. The manuscript is dated October 17, 1830.

Giaour - One outside the Moslem faith.

Page 83

Vasily Dmitrievich Sukhorukov (1795-1841), journalist and historian. His material for a history of the Don Cossacks had been confiscated after the Decembrist rebellion, and he was sent to the Caucasus. He then collected material for a history of the campaign of 1828-29, but was arrested again in 1828 (for keeping company with former Decembrists), sent to Finland, and again relieved of his material. Pushkin tried unsuccessfully to help him regain his papers. The history of the war was eventually (1836) published by Nikolai Ivanovich Ushakov (1802-61), a military historian who used Sukhorukov's material without giving his name. The book was called *A History of the Military Activities in Asian Turkey in 1828 and 1829 (Istoriia voennykh deistvii v Aziatskoi Turtsii v 1828 i 1829 godakh).*

Bey-Bulat Taimazov, leader of the tribal warfare in the Caucasus. In 1828 he went over to the Russians and served thereafter as a guarantee for safe passage along the Georgian Military Highway.

Page 84

A*** has sometimes been thought to be I. Ia. Abramovich who had served with Paskevich. However, at this time he was not at the front.

Page 87

Peter Petrovich Konovnitsyn (1802-30) was sent to Siberia and the Caucasus after the Decembrist rebellion.

Page 90

Rufin Ivanovich Dorokhov (died 1852), well-known duelist who often lost his military rank because of this pastime. He served in the Nizhegorod Regiment of Dragoons. Prototype of Dolokhov in Tolstoy's *War and Peace.*

Russian magazines - The article in question was by Nikolai Ivanovich Nadezhdin (Nikodim Nadoumko) [1804-56] on Pushkin's narrative poem *Poltava,* and was published in the *Messenger of Europe (Vestnik Evropy),* No. 8 and No. 9, 1829. The article is written in the form of a comedy where the actors are the author (a classicist), a romantic, and an old university press proof reader. Pushkin has only kept the latter, instead supplying the deacon and the maker of communion bread.

Zdravomysl - "Common sense."

Acknowledgements

—First of all to Richard Burgi, who made numerous useful suggestions about the translation, and whom I find a most inspiring teacher and person;

—Also to Clarence F. Brown, who suggested the need for a translation of the *Journey* and kindly read it;

—To Sonja Bargmann, William E. Bown, Andrew G. Jones, David H. Miller, and Norman A. Moscowitz, who read all or parts of the manuscript and offered many helpful ideas;

—Also to Ron E. Openshaw; Far, B. Ewert C. Ingemanson; and W. Malcolm Henry for their support and encouragement.